Kali Linux: 2 Books in 1

The Complete Beginner's Guide About Kali Linux For Beginners & Hacking With Kali Linux, Full of Practical Examples Of Wireless Networking & Penetration Testing.

© Copyright 2019 by **Learn Computer Hacking In Deep** - All rights reserved.

This eBook is provided with the sole purpose of providing relevant information on a specific topic for which every reasonable effort has been made to ensure that it is both accurate and reasonable. Nevertheless, by purchasing this eBook you consent to the fact that the author, as well as the publisher, are in no way experts on the topics contained herein, regardless of any claims as such that may be made within. As such, any suggestions or recommendations that are made within are done so purely for entertainment value. It is recommended that you always consult a professional prior to undertaking any of the advice or techniques discussed within.

This is a legally binding declaration that is considered both valid and fair by both the Committee of Publishers Association and the American Bar Association and should be considered as legally binding within the United States.

The reproduction, transmission, and duplication of any of the content found herein, including any specific or extended information will be done as an illegal act regardless of the end from the information ultimately takes. This includes copied versions of the work both physical, digital and audio unless express consent of the Publisher is provided beforehand. Any additional rights reserved.

Furthermore, the information that can be found within the pages described forthwith shall be considered both accurate and truthful when it comes to the recounting of facts. As such, any use, correct or incorrect, of the provided information will render the Publisher free of responsibility as to the actions taken outside of their direct purview. Regardless, there are zero scenarios where the original author or the Publisher can be deemed liable in any fashion for any damages or hardships that may result from any of the information discussed herein.

Additionally, the information in the following pages is intended only for informational purposes and should thus be thought of as universal. As befitting its nature, it is presented without assurance regarding its prolonged validity or interim quality Trademarks that are mentioned are done without written consent and can in no way be considered an endorsement from the trademark holder.

Table of Contents

Introduction 2

Chapter 1: Installing and Downloading Kali Linux 4

Chapter 2: Troubleshooting Installations 9

Chapter 3: Kali Linux External Boot Drive 14

Chapter 4: Basics 18

Chapter 5: Real World Application of Kali Linux and Other Useful Tools 56

Chapter 6: Programming Linux 61

Chapter 7: Basics of Networking 91

Chapter 8: Proxies and Proxy Chains 95

Chapter 9: Virtual Private Networks 100

Chapter 10: Introduction to Wireless Networking 104

Conclusion 120

Chapter 1: Kali History 133

Chapter 2: Hard Drive Installation 141

Chapter 3: Well-Suited Package Handling Utility 155

Chapter 4: Tarballas 165

Chapter 5: A Practical Guide to Installing Nessus 171

Chapter 6: Including a Repository Source 203

Chapter 7: Metasploitable 214

Chapter 8: Start with the Target's Own Website 232

Chapter 9: Scanning 252

Conclusion 256

If you love listening to audio books on-the-go, I have great news for you. You can download the audio book version of this book for FREE just by signing up for a FREE 30-day audible trial! See below for more details!

As an audible customer, you will receive the below benefits with your 30-day free trial:

- FREE audible book copy of this book
- After the trial, you will get 1 credit each month to use on any audiobook
- Your credits automatically roll over to the next month if you don't use them
- Choose from Audible's 200,000 + titles
- Listen anywhere with the Audible app across multiple devices
- Make easy, no-hassle exchanges of any audiobook you don't love
- Keep your audiobooks forever, even if you cancel your membership
- And much more

Click the links below to get started!

For Audible US

For Audible UK

For Audible FR

For Audible DE

Kali Linux

BOOK 1

Kali Linux

Introduction

Congratulations on downloading the eBook copy of *"Kali Linux for Beginners: Computer Hacking & Programming Guide with Practical Examples of Wireless Networking Hacking & Penetration Testing with Kali Linux to Understand the Basics of Cybersecurity"*. I am really delighted to see that you have shown great interest in getting to know about the basics of Kali Linux along with all its usefulness in the world of technology today. It can be regarded among the most effective software in today's world. Many even regard Kali Linux as a great boon for the people concerned with computing and networking.

Kali Linux functions as a software for auditing of security and also works from the perspective of networking and hacking. This powerful software comes packed up with lots of security along with information based tasks like security research, reverse engineering and penetration testing. Computer forensics is also a part of this software.

This software is a member of the Linux family. Linux distribution is primarily concerned with cyber security. Most of the big companies today seek the help of Kali Linux for the purpose of tracing and checking the various forms of vulnerabilities which are present within a system. Kali Linux falls under the category of open-source program and it is absolutely free. Kali Linux is a 100% legal software and it is being used for a variety of scenarios within organizations.

Kali Linux

Every effort has been made towards making this book as interesting as possible. Hope you can gain a wide amount of knowledge about Kali Linux. Enjoy!

Kali Linux

Chapter 1: Installing and Downloading Kali Linux

If you want to opt for information security as your career choice, the most important thing that you will need is to install an operating system which mainly functions as a security system administrator. A proper OS will help you in performing the variety of tasks related to information security and will make the time-consuming jobs very easy. In today's world of information security, you can find a wide range of operating systems among which Kali Linux is regarded as the best of all.

It works as a great tool for the purpose of penetration testing and information security. Today, it is being used by most penetration testers along with ethical hackers who are concerned with the security of a system as well as with various other assessments of the network.

Among all other distributions of Linux, Kali Linux is one of the finest and leading distribution which is being widely used today in the world of security auditing. Kali Linux is the one and only operating system which is related to the security of networks and ethical hacking. It comes with loads of tools which are related to command line hacking which is necessary for various jobs related to the information security.

Kali Linux is most commonly used for computer forensics, security of system application, and penetration testing along with network security. Kali Linux is also the prime OS designed for the purpose of ethical hacking.

Kali Linux

How to download Kali Linux?

Kali Linux is an open-source software. That means that the OS can be used and utilized completely along with being totally free. So, Kali Linux can be downloaded easily from the official website of the OS. You can install it by various techniques which you can find in the next section. You will come across various versions of the same and you can install the one which meets your needs.

While downloading the installation file, you will also come across some numbers in hexadecimal number which are being used for the purpose of security jobs. You need to properly check out the integrity of the image which you have downloaded. You will also need to check the SHA-256 fingerprint of the installation file.

How to install Kali Linux on your computer?

The overall process related to the installation of Kali Linux on your computer is super easy. You can choose any of the options which are available for installing the OS. The most commonly used installation options are:

- Installing the OS with the use a of hard drive.
- Installing the OS with the help of Kali Linux bootable USB drive.
- Installing the OS with the help of VMware or VirtualBox.
- Installing the OS with the help of dual booting.

Kali Linux

Among all the options which are available for installing Kali Linux on your system, installing the OS with the help of VirtualBox and by using bootable USB drive is the most common. Your system requires a minimum of 20GB of free hard drive space along with a minimum of 4 GB RAM in case you want to install the OS with the use of VMware or VirtualBox.

Installation of Kali Linux with the help of virtualization software

- Just before starting with the process of installation, you need to install a virtualization software like VMware. You can also choose other options such as
- VirtualBox which is a product of Oracle. After you are done with installing the virtualization software launch the software from the applications folder.
- You need to download the installation file for the OS which you can easily get from the official website. After that, launch the virtual machine. For this, open up the home page of the virtualization software which you have installed on your system and then choose Create New Virtual Machine from the options.
- After you are done with creating a new virtual machine, select the iso file or image of the Kali Linux OS which needs to be followed by the selection of guest operating system. You also need to configure each and every detail related to the virtual machine, like Kali Linux. You can now easily start the virtual machine related to Kali Linux after

- selecting the Kali Linux VM. After you have selected the VM, click on the green button Power button.
- Right after the VM has been powered up, you will see a pop-up menu where you need to select your required installation mode in the menu of GRUB. Select the option of Graphical Installation and then select Continue.
- The succeeding screens will be asking you to determine the information related to locale such as your preferred language in which you want to use Kali Linux, your location, keyboard layout and others.
- After you are done with all these, you will need to set up a strong password for the Kali Linux VM. Followed by this, the installer will be asking you to select the time zone and then will pause at the step of disk partition. You can either choose Entire Disk Space or Create Separate Partition for the VM.
- You will need to save all the changes but do not continue with the process as it will completely erase all the data which is present on the disk. So, always confirm the settings first before proceeding further.
- After this, you will be asked to install the GRUB boot loader. Select Yes and then choose the device for saving up the information of the boot loader which is needed for booting up the Kali Linux VM.
- Click on Finish and the installer will finish the final stage procedures.

Kali Linux

- The OS can also be installed by the help of a bootable USB drive as well.

Chapter 2: Troubleshooting Installations

Kali Linux has turned out to be a quite reliable software when it comes to penetration testing and ethical hacking. But, there are times when the system fails and it becomes a tiresome job to install the same. There can be a wide range of possibilities behind the failure of Kali Linux installation. This could include problems like incomplete or corrupted iso download, insufficient disk space of the target machine and many others.

The installer of Kali Linux is really reliable but facing bugs or encountering external problems like bad mirrors, network problems, etc. is very common. So, all that you need to do in such situations is to simply troubleshoot the process of installation so that you can proceed.

Whenever the installer of Kali Linux fails, it comes up with a screen which shows "Installation Step Failed". At such a point, you need to know that the Kali Linux installer functions with various virtual consoles: the primary screen which you can see runs either on fifth console (for the installer of graphics use CTRL+Alt+F5) or on the first console (for the installer of texts use Shift+F4).

In both of these cases, the fourth console which can be seen by CTRL+Shift+F4 will help in displaying all the related logs of what exactly is happening within the installer. You can easily evaluate the reason for the installer problem with a more detailed error message such as "the log screen of installer" which indicates that the target machine is running out of space and the installer is unable to proceed with the step.

The log screen of the installer

The third and the second consoles, which are CTRL+Shift+F3 and CTRL+Shift+F2 respectively, host the shells which can be used for further investigation of the present situation in complete detail. Most of the tools of the command line are provided by BusyBox and so the set of features is somewhat limited. They are enough for figuring out the majority of the problems which you are most likely to encounter during the installation of Kali Linux.

As you click on Continue, which is available on the main screen Installation Failure, the installer will return you to a screen which you are not likely to see in normal conditions, the Main Menu of the Kali Linux installer. This screen will let you launch the steps of the installation one by one. If you can manage to mend the problem with the help of the installer shell access you can easily start again with the step which failed.

What can you do in the shell of installer

With the installer shell, you can easily inspect and also modify the database of debconf with the commands debconf-get and debconf-set. These commands are used for the purpose of testing the preceeding values. You can check any of the files like the complete log of installation, available in /var/log/syslog with more or cat. You can also edit any of the files with nano along with the files which are being installed on the system.

Main Menu of the Kali Linux installer

In case you are still not able to resolve the installation problem, you can file a report of the bug. The report of the bug needs to include the logs of the installer which can be easily retrieved with the Save Debug Logs option available from the main menu.

With this, you can export the logs in various ways, like in mounted file system, floppy or on the web. The most convenient way of saving the debug logs is to let the Kali Linux installer start with a hosting of the web server for the log files. You can launch a web browser from any other computer which is also in the same network and then download all the available log files.

Other methods of troubleshooting

There are various other simple ways to troubleshoot the installation of Kali Linux. Let's have a look at them.

- **Downloading the official form of Kali Linux image:** Make sure that you have downloaded the ISO file for Kali Linux from the official website. The image files are available in various formats such as ISO files, ARM images and VMware images. The ISO files are available in two formats: 32 bits and 64 bits. The VMware images come pre-installed with the VMware virtual machine. The image of VMware is available in the format of 32 bit PAE. In the case of ARM images, it is not at all possible to have one format of image which will be working across all the devices of ARM. In the Kali Linux website, you can find ARM images for various devices such as rk3306 mk/ss808, ODROID-U2/X2, Samsung Chromebook, Raspberry Pi and various others.

- **Verify the checksums of SHA1 for the downloaded images:** While downloading the image for Kali Linux, make sure that you check the SHA1SUMS.gpg and SHA1SUMS file which is available right next to the images of download. Before verifying the image checksums, be sure that SHA1SUMS file is the only one which has been generated by Kali.
- **Installation steps verification:** If you are installing Kali Linux using DVD, try to burn the DVD at the slowest speed. Make sure that you have disabled the firewall or antivirus on the system so that it does not interrupt the writing process. If you are facing a low disk space error, try to increase the allocated space of the disk. Check the space which you have allocated for the installation of Kali Linux. The best option is to allocate at least 20 GB of space along with the space of swap. You can also troubleshoot the installation by deleting and

Kali Linux

then repartitioning the free space on the disk. You can also allow the installer itself to partition the free space on the disk automatically and this might resolve your problem.

Kali Linux

Chapter 3: Kali Linux External Boot Drive

Kali Linux is a well-renowned name in the world of information security. It has been funded and maintained by Offensive Security which is a provider of services related to penetration testing and information security. Kali Linux has become a go-to distribution for the purpose of hacking. Within a few minutes, you can have a functioning box of pen testing along with various sets of tools that you can find anywhere else. Kali Linux comes pre-installed with a wide array of tools which reduces the stress of installing other tools.

Various options available for running Kali Linux

You can have the option of installing Kali Linux completely on your system. But, in most cases, the systems which you need for the purpose of Penetration testing or ethical hacking might require you to still keep Windows or any other OS as the primary form of operating system. In such cases, what you are left with is to use a virtualization tool and then use the same for running Kali Linux within a virtual machine. However, if there is a lack of memory in the system running on Windows or any
other OS, it might result in crashing the VM frequently. Another option is to run Kali Linux on an external USB drive with Kali Linux installed on it. The only problem that comes with this option is the lack of encryption.

What is the best option?

Kali Linux

Installing and then running Kali Linux from an encrypted form of external bootable USB drive is regarded as the best option.

But, you also need to secure the same. So, for doing that, you need to follow these steps.

- Start by using a USB drive which is owned by the concerned company.
- Perform full installation of Kali Linux to 1 TB USB drive by using complete encryption of disk on the drive.
- You then need to encrypt the data on the USB drive. As the onboard drive is also in the encrypted state by using a different form of encryption, the onboard drive will not be accessible as well at the time of booting to the OS which is working from the USB drive.
- As the USB drive which you are using is owned by the company, the all-over data which is used is stored in the hardware of the concerned company.
- After the entire project is over, you can hand over the external USB drive to the company and all the related information of testing and data is returned to the client.

Getting started with Kali Linux on USB drive

To start the process, you need to download the ISO file of the Kali Linux installer and then burn the image to the external USB drive you are using. Insert the external USB drive into the machine on which you are going to run

Kali Linux

Kali Linux. Make sure that you insert the USB drive into the system before booting the system.

- **Setting up the drive:** The next step that you need to follow is to set up the drive, encrypting and then partitioning the same. A dialog box will appear which will be asking you to choose the partition type which you want for the installation. Opt for Guided-Use Entire Disk for the best performance. This also helps in fully encrypting the USB drive when compared to just encrypting the directory of /home. Always remember that the tools of Kali Linux store all the data in various other places other than the home directory at the time of penetration testing.

  The next screen will be asking you to choose the disk on which you want to install it. At this point, make sure that you pick the desired USB drive to install Kali Linux and not on any local drive of the system. If you select any of the local drives, you will be wiping the OS from that particular drive. After you have selected the USB drive click on Continue.

- The next window will be asking you how to partition the USB drive. Select All Files on one partition and click on Continue.

- Next, you will be asked to save all the information of partition and then the process of partitioning the drive will start. When you select continue, all the data on the USB drive will be erased. So, before clicking on Continue, select the Yes option.

Kali Linux

- The process of disk encryption will start along with the process of partitioning. The drive is completely erased first and then encrypted. This entire process will take a while. If you are using a USB drive of 64 GB, it will take 30 minutes to get encrypted. If you are using a 1 TB USB drive, it will take approximately 10 hours for encryption.
- After the process is complete, you will be asked to provide a passphrase which will be used for encryption. Make sure that you use a strong one as this will be used at the time of booting up Kali Linux.
- Next, confirm the changes and then select Finish Partitioning.
- Now the system will begin the process of partitioning and after the process has been completed, the installation system will start.
- You will also be asked if you want to use any Network Mirror. Click on Yes as this will be selecting the repo mirrors which are nearby your location and will also help in speeding up the process of update later.

Booting Kali Linux

Insert the USB drive into the machine and then start it up. At the booting process, open up the boot menu and select the USB drive which you want to use. Now you will be required to enter the passphrase and after successful entry, the system will start.

Chapter 4: Basics

Before we start with other aspects of Kali Linux, it is necessary for you to learn about some of the basic tools and commands that come with Linux. Let's have a look at some of the most basic components.

Essential Linux Terminal Commands

In relation to the other operating systems which are available in the market and Linux in particular, when it comes to the term Command, it means a line of command for the applications or the functionalities which are built into the shell of the user. However, this distinction is of very little consequence for the end-users.

. Both of them are used in the same way. You need to input the words into the emulator of your terminal and it will provide results as outputs.

Linux commands for management of file system

- **ls:** This command helps in listing all the contents in the current directory. When you provide the same with a path, it will list the specific contents of that path only. Some of the useful options that you need to know are –l and –a, it displays information as a long list format which comes with much more detailed information and also shows the dot or hidden files.

Kali Linux

- **cat:** When provided with one single file, this command helps in printing the contents of that file to the output in standard style. When you provide the command with many files at a time, it concatenates them and then the output is redirected into a completely new file. The most useful is the option of –n which helps in numbering the lines.

- **cd:** This command helps in jumping from the present directory to some other specified directory. When you use this command without any argument, it will return to the home directory. When you use this command with two dots such as 'cd..' it will return you to the directory which is right above the present one and using the command with a dash such as 'cd –' will return to the directory just before the current one, regardless of the location in relation to the present directory.

- **pwd:** This command helps in printing the current directory. This command is very useful when your prompt does not contain this specific information. It is very useful for BASH programming which is used for obtaining the directory reference of the one in which you are going to execute the code.

- **mkdir:** This command is used for the purpose of creating new directories. The most handy form of switch is –p which helps by creating an entire structure of specific nature if it is not present already.

Kali Linux

- **file:** The command file helps in indicating the file type. As the files in a Linux system are not under any form of obligation for having the extensions related to the system to work, it becomes hard for users to get the exact type of a file at times. This command helps in solving this form of problem related to Linux.

- **cp:** This command copies all the directories and files. As this command does not copy the directories recurrently by default, always remember to use –a or –r with this command. The –a command helps in preserving the ownership, mode and time stamp besides copying.

- **mv:** It is used for renaming or moving directories and files. Renaming and moving can be regarded as one single operation where renaming is just moving one single file to the same place with a different name.

- **rm:** The 'rm' command is used to delete directories and files. It is a very essential command that you need to know as you will not be able to remove any clutter without this command. However, while using this command you must be super attentive as this command permanently deletes the files and directories. Unlike other commands, this command does not even store the deleted files and directories somewhere else from where you can fish them out after. Once they are gone, they are gone forever. So, in such cases, using the –r switch is very essential along with the command.

Kali Linux

- **ln:** This command is used for creating symbolic or hard links in between the files. The soft or symbolic links are somewhat like the shortcuts of Windows which provides a very easy way of accessing any particular folder or file.
- **chmod:** It helps in changing the permissions of users. By permissions it includes writing, viewing and executing files. Any user can change the user permission for the files which he/she owns.
- **chown:** This command is used for changing the ownership of the files. Only the root user is able to use this command and can change the file ownership. For the purpose of recursively changing the ownership for all the files within a directory, you can use the command with –R.
- **find:** This command is used for searching the entire filesystem for some specific directories or files. This command is very powerful in nature not just because of its capabilities of searching but because this command allows the users to execute any arbitrary form of commands on the non-matching or matching files.
- **locate:** Opposite to 'find,' 'locate' command searches the database for the patterns of the file names. This form of database consists of the snapshots of the entire filesystem.
- **du:** The 'du' command is used for showing the directory or file size. Among the various useful options are –s which provides a summary in place of an entire listing, -h which converts the reported sizes to a

- **df:** This command is used for showing the usage of disk. The default output of this command lists each and every filesystem, reports the sizes of the same and also the used space along with the space which is available. You can add on –h with this command for getting the report in a more human-friendly format.
- **dd:** This command helps in converting and copying a specific file in accordance to the main page. You need to provide this command with the source and the destination and it will copy the files respectively.
- **mount/unmount:** This command pair performs the function of mounting and unmounting the filesystems. This whole thing can even range from USB sticks to the ISO images.

Linux commands for processing of text

- **more/less:** These two commands are somewhat similar in function and allow the user to easily view the texts chunked as screenfuls. Suppose there is a very large output from some of the commands, like cat for a file and the emulator took some time to scroll the entire text. When you use any of these commands, you can scroll the texts easily now. The command 'less' is newer when compared to 'more' so 'more' is not used now.

- **head/tail:** This is also a pair of commands but in this, both have their individual uses. The command 'head' helps in outputting one number from the first line of a file and the 'tail' command helps by providing output as a number from the last line of any file. The default output number of these commands is ten which can be controlled by using the option –n. Another switch which can be used with this command is –f.
- **grep:** This command helps by searching the texts for the patterns. By default function, this command looks at the standard input but the users can easily specify the files which are meant to be searched. The pattern can either be a regular expression or a normal string. It can also print out either matching or non-matching lines along with the contexts of the same. When you run a command which provides lots of information as output, just use this command and see the magic.
- **sort:** This command is used for sorting the text lines according to various criteria. The useful switches which can be used along with this command are –n which helps in sorting the numeric values of any string, -r which helps in reversing the provided output and various others. You can use this command while sorting the output of

'du' command when you want the files sorted in the descending order exactly according to the sizes of the same.

- **wc:** The 'wc' command is used for counting the words, the lines, the bytes and characters.
- **diff:** This command helps in showing the exact difference between two different files using line by line comparison.

Linux commands for management of the process

- **kill/xkill/pkill/killall:** All of these commands are used for the purpose of killing any process and then terminating it. The difference between all these lies in what they accept as inputs. The 'kill' command accepts the ID of process, the 'xkill' command allows the user to click on a window for closing the same and 'killall' along with 'pkill' accepts only the names of the processes.
- **ps/pgrep:** It has already been mentioned in the previous command that 'kill' requires the ID of the process. This can be obtained by using the command 'ps' which helps in printing the information related to the current processes which are active in nature. The command 'pgrep' works in a particular way: you are required to provide the name of the process and it will return the process ID.

Kali Linux

- **top/htop:** These two commands are similar in function and both of these help in displaying the processes. It can also be thought of as the monitors of a console system.
- **time:** This command works as a process. You can think of this as the stopwatch for the execution of a program.

Linux commands for User and BASH environment

- **su/sudo:** Both of these commands are different ways of achieving the same thing- running the commands as some other user. Completely depending on the type of distribution that you have, you have seen one or the other but in actual both are serviceable with these commands. The difference between two commands is that 'su' switches the user to some different user whereas 'sudo' runs the commands only with the privileges of other users.
- **date:** Unlike the command 'time,' this command helps in printing the time along with the date for the standard form of output. The output can also be formatted according to the user specification and it includes everything: month, day and year.
- **alias:** This command helps in creating and changing the aliases to some other commands. This means that you can easily provide new names to new commands or you can rename the already existing

commands. It is very useful for the purpose of abbreviating the long command strings which can cause problems while memorizing.

- **uname:** It helps in outputting some of the basic information about the system. By pairing this command with –a you can get the kernel information along with the hostname and architecture of the processor.
- **uptime:** This command will tell you the duration for which the system has been running. It is not very important but it helps in finding out the overall time of the system processing.
- **sleep:** This command helps in shutting down the system after a specific period of time.

Linux commands for management of user

- **useradd, usermod, userdel:** All of these commands will help you to add, modify and delete the accounts of the users. In case you are the only sole user of the system, you will not be requiring these commands that much. But, if the system is being used by various users at a time then these commands are very useful.
- **passwd:** This command will allow you to change the password of your user account. As the root user, you can reset all the normal nature of user passwords however you cannot view the passwords. It is of utter importance to change the passwords from time to time.

Kali Linux

Linux commands for documentation/help

- **man / whatis:** The command 'man' helps by bringing up the manual for one specific command. The majority of the command lines come with man page. The command 'whatis' helps by providing one line summary of some specific section of the manual.
- **whereis:** This command tells the users where the binary files of executable nature lives, provided that the binary files are within the path of the user. It can also find out the source code and manual page, if present.

Linux commands for networking

- **ip:** This command helps by providing the ip address of a system.
- **ping:** The 'ping' command functions as an important tool of diagnosis. It helps in testing easily whether you are connected with the internet or router. It also helps by indicating the connection quality.

Linux Command Line

Command line can be regarded as one of the strengths of Linux systems. The CLI or command line interface allows the user to be absolutely free of the distros. It also makes the task of interacting with the system much easier. The derivate of Ubuntu uses the same base of codes but all of them come with a completely different set of tools for performing the same job. The various forms of desktop environments on the similar distro will require various ways toperform the same form of task. As a user, you will need to forget the processes that you already know and then re-learn the processes for performing the same thing as they hop between the distros. The command line of Linux saves the resources of the system which are also consumed by the GUIs. So, in case you are working on a slower system, it is better for you to use command line rather than GUI.

Many people think of command line as being very difficult; however, it is not. It is as simple as messaging your friends where you text the system what to do.

Getting the shell

Shell is nothing but a program which turns the typed text into the form of orders or commands for the computer system to perform. You can use various forms of commands for performing the same task. There are various shells which you can find for Linux but the most popular shell of all is the BASH, written by the GNU Project. . Another form of modern-day shell is the 'zsh' which you can easily install for your distribution.

If you are working on a desktop environment, you will require a terminal emulator for the purpose of emulating the terminal within the particular

Kali Linux

interface. Different form of distros come with their own emulators: KDE comes along with Konsole and Gnome also comes along with Gnome terminal.

Some of the basic commands

When you open up the terminal emulator, you will be in the home directory by default of the user who is logged in. You can easily find out the name of the user who is logged in along with the hostname. The '$' indicates that you have logged in as a regular form of user whereas the '#' indicates that you have been logged in as the root. Unless and until you are doing any form of administrative tasks or functioning outside the directories of root, never function as root.

This will change all the permissions for all the directories along with the files on which you have already worked on and will make the root the user of all those directories. You can easily list all the available directories along with the files inside them by using the command '/s.'

If you need to change any of the directories, use the command 'cd.' You can also employ the key 'tab' which helps by auto-completing the complete path. You can use forward slash for the purpose of entering the directories. You will not need to provide the entire path in case you want to get inside the sub-directory of the present directory. For seeing the contents of a directory, you will not need to change the directory. Just use the command 'ls' for viewing the contents of a specific directory.

Kali Linux

Some Advanced Command Line

Most of the developers who work with the command line of Linux know the basic form of commands such as 'cd,' 'ls,' 'tail,' 'head,' 'cat,' 'grep,' 'find,' 'sort' and many others. The advanced users will need to know how to function with the beasts such as 'awk' and 'sed' or even perl-oneliners. With advanced knowledge of BASH scripting, you will find that imagination is the only limit. Let's have a look at some of the advanced form of command line.

- **watch:** This command performs as a very beautiful program which periodically executes a program and also outputs the contents of the same on full screen. In case you place the command within inside quotes, you can also run more than one command at a time such as watch –n 1 ' ls –la ; echo ; vmstat ; echo; df '. This whole command will be executing a full listing, displaying the statistics of memory along with the disk space. All of these will be separated with empty lines and will repeat after every second. It is a great way of watching large files get copied and also keeping an eye on the disk space so that it does not come up with any form of issue.
- **curl:** Most of the PHP developers are acquainted with the cURL extension of php which is also available for the command line of Linux. In place of writing any other additional program of php, you can simply use this command line. All the options which you will

- need are available. Enter 'man curl' and you can find out all the possible tools.
- **logsave:** This tool is very important in nature and it helps by capturing the output from a program and then sends the same as a log file. It also adds a timestamp of beginning and end. You can add up the '–a' parameter for appending the log file.
- **lsof:** This command stands for list open files. It displays all the files which the system has opened up currently. It is very helpful for figuring out which processes use one certain file or also for displaying all the available files for one single process.
- **strace:** The 'strace' command helps by tracing all the calls of the system which are made by a particular program to the kernel of Linux. This indicates that you can see when a program is opened, closed, read, writes, access the files and many others. It is somewhat like running an entire program without any form of cover. For example, 'strace –ff –e trace=open /usr/sbin/apache 2' will strace the apache2 program and will also output all the open calls.
- **z* tools:** You will often need to diff, grep or cat the files which are compressed. In place of the unpacked files, you can treat the files as being unpacked already simply by using the command 'zgrep' in place of grep, 'zdiff' in place of diff and 'zcat' in place of cat and various others.

Kali Linux

- **iconv:** This command helps in converting a file which is encoded in one way for converting the same in some other format.
- **nc:** This command is capable of doing everything and can also be used for checking the requests of service and for making sure that the correct headers have been sent out.

Finding Stuff

Most of the people use graphical file manager for finding out the files in Linux like Nautilus in Gnome, Thunar in Xfce and Dolphin in KDE. However, you can also use the command line for finding out various stuff in Linux which does not even depend on the type of desktop manager that you use.

By using the command 'find'

The command 'find' will allow you to search for the files for which you already know the probable filenames. The command in its simplest form searches for all the files within the present directory and then through the sub-directories of the same depending on your search criteria. You can search out for the files by using the name, group, owner, type, date, permissions and various other criteria. Enter a dot (.) after the command as 'find.' which will be listing all the files in the present directory which has been found. In order to find a file which matches with some particular pattern, you can use the argument

Kali Linux

'–name.' You can provide the metacharacters of the filename like * but you will need to put '\' in front of them or enclose the same within quotes. In case the find command cannot locate any of the files which are matching with your criteria, it will produce no output.

Using the command 'locate'

The command 'locate' is much faster when compared to 'find' as it employs a past built database, where the command 'find' searches within the real system along all the actual files and directories.

This command returns a large list of all the names of the paths which also contains the specific character groups. The simplest form of this command finds out all the files within the file system which starts at the root. In case you want to find all the directories or files which contains the proper and only the criteria of search which you have provided, use the argument '–b' along with the command as: locate –b '\yourdata'. The backslash which has been used in the command line acts as a globbing character which gives a way for expanding the characters of wildcard within a file name of non-specific nature into a set of filenames of specific nature.

A wildcard is nothing but a symbol which can be easily replaced by one or more than one characters when the overall expression is being evaluated. The most widely used form of wildcard symbols are '?' which indicates one single character and '*' which indicates a long string of characters. The command 'mlocate' is a new form of the 'locate' command. It helps in indexing the complete file system. However, the results of search include only the files which the current user has access to. Whenever you update the database of 'mlocate,' it will keep the timestamp information within the database.

Using the command 'which'

This command returns the exact path of the executable which is being called when any command is issued.

The 'which' command is very useful for finding out the location of any executable for the purpose of creating a shortcut of the program on the user desktop, on any panel or on some other place within the desktop manager. The 'which' command by default will only display the first executable which is matching. For the purpose of displaying all the executables which are matching, you need to use the option '–a' along with the command.

Modifying Files

One of the many things that Linux along with various operating systems provides is the tools needed to create as well as for edit the text files. There are various text editors that can be found today and every Linux user has their personal favorite. Let's have a look at some of the most famous text file editors in Linux.

Kali Linux

Text editors

If you are a Windows user then you must be familiar with the classic text editor known as Notepad. Linux also offers users somewhat similar programs such as gedit, NEdit and geany. All of these programs are absolutely free and each provides more or less the same service. Such programs come with the facility of syntax highlighting which readily helps in editing the source code along with the documents which are written in any markup language like CSS or HTML.

- **NEdit:** This is a form of straightforward text editor which is more or less like the Windows Notepad. It comes with Motif-style of the interface.
- **Geany:** It is a Linux text editor which is not similar to the Notepad++ from Windows. It comes along with a tabbed form of interface for the purpose of working with various open files at one time and also comes with other features such as displaying the line numbers in one margin. It uses up the interface toolkit of GTK+.
- **Gedit:** This is the default form of text editor for the GNOME desktop environment. It is one of the best text editors which can be easily used on any type of Linux based system.

Kali Linux

Text editors based on terminal

When you are working from the Linux CLI, you have a wide range of choice in text editors. Let's have a look at some of them.

- **pico:** This text editor started off as the editor which was built in the email program which was also text based known as pine. This text editor was eventually packaged as one stand-alone program for editing and modifying the text files. The modern-day version of this text editor is known as alpine. On the system based on Linux, you can install this text editor by using the command: sudo apt-get install alpine-pico.
- **nano:** This can be regarded as the GNU version of the text editor pico and can be taken as the similar program under a completely different name. You can install nano on any Linux based system by using the command: sudo apt-get install nano.
- **vim:** This stands for 'vi improved' and it functions as a text editor which is also used by the majority of computer professionals. The controls of this text editor might feel a bit confusing the first time. As you become familiar with it, it can make the execution of the most complex editing tasks very fast and easy. If you want to install vim on any system which is based on Linux use the command: sudo apt-get install vim.

- **emacs:** This is a very complex and highly customizable form of text editor which comes with a built-in interpreter meant for the Lisp programming language. It is specifically used by computer professionals who work in the dialects of Lisp like Scheme. If you are required to install emacs on your Linux based system, use the command: sudo apt-get install emacs.

Redirecting the command output into text file

When you are using Linux command line, you might sometimes need to create or even make changes to any text file without running a text editor in actual. Here are some of the commands which you can use for this purpose.

Creating empty file with the command touch

For the purpose of creating an empty file, you can use the touch command. This command helps in updating the mtime and atime attributes of the file assuming that the file contents have been changed whereas nothing actually changes. When you touch any file which does not even exist in actual, the system will be creating that file without putting any form of data inside the file. You can use the command like: touch myfile.txt. This command will be creating a new and empty file named as myfile.txt only if that file does not exist already.

Kali Linux

Redirecting text into any file

Sometimes you might need to stick the resulting output of a command into a specific file. For accomplishing this motive easily, you need to use the symbol '>' for redirecting the resulting output to some specific file. For example, the command echo is being used for echoing text as the output. So, the command will be: echo "example text". This command will print the text on your screen and then will return to the command prompt. For redirecting this same output to a file you can use >. For example, echo "example text">myfile.txt. This will be putting the text "example text" into a file named as myfile.txt. In case the file myfile.txt does not exist, it will be created by the system. In case it already exists, all the contents of that file will be overwritten; it will destroy the previous contents of that file and replace it with the new text.

Redirecting to the end of any file

The operator of redirect >> is somewhat similar to the >. However, in place of just overwriting the contents of a file, this command appends the brand new data to the end position of that file. For example, ls –l>>directory.txt. This command will be taking the output from ls-l and then will add it to the file directory.txt. If the file does not exist, it will be created by the system. If it already exists in the system, the output of ls-l will be attached to the file end, after one line of the already existing file contents.

Kali Linux

Adding and Removing Software

If you have been using a Linux based system for a long time, you must have known that there are ways of doing the same thing in Linux. This includes installing software applications onto a machine based on Linux by using the command line. The majority of the Linux based users opt for the CLI to install new software in the system. Among the most commonly used methods for installing the software from the CLI is via the software repositories which is where the software files are stored. It is done by using package manager. All the software based on Linux is being distributed as packages which are nothing but files which are associated with the management system of packages. Each and every distribution of Linux comes along with a management system for the packages, however, all of them are not the same.

What is the package management system?

Package management systems consists of a set of tools along with various file formats which are utilized together for installing, updating and uninstalling Linux based software. The two most commonly found systems of package management are from Debian and Red Hat. CentOS, Red Hat and Fedora use the rpm system of files in which the files are in the .rpm format while Ubuntu, Mint and Debian use the dpkg system of files in which the files are in the .deb format. The main difference of all these systems is the way you are going to install and maintain them.

Kali Linux

The inside contents of the .deb or .rpm files are somewhat like the old files of archive like the .zip which contains the code of the applications, the methods of installing the software, the dependencies and the location of where the configuration files need to be placed. The software which executes and reads all of the above mentioned instructions is known as the package manager.

Ubuntu, Debian, Mint and various others

Ubuntu, Debian, Mint and the rest of the Debian based distributions use the .deb format of files, along with the dpkg system of package management. There are two different ways of installing the applications through this system.

You can employ the apt application to install the repository or you can also use the dpkg applications to install the apps from the .deb files. Let's see how to perform both the functions.

Installing the applications by using the apt command is very easy:

$ sudo apt upgrade

If you want to update only one application:

Kali Linux

$ sudo apt update app_name

In case the application which you want to install in the system is not readily available within the repository of Debian and is available as .deb download:

$ sudo dpkg –i app_name.deb

Red Hat, Fedora and CentOS

Red Hat uses various systems of package management, by default. All these systems use their own terminologies but are still somewhat similar to each other and with the ones which are used in Debian. For instance, you can use either dnf or yum manager for installing the applications.

$ sudo yum install app_name
$ sudo dnf install app_name

The applications which are in the .rpm format can also be upgraded in the system with the help of the rpm command.

$ sudo rpm –i app_name.rpm

If you want to remove some of the unwanted applications from the system then:

Kali Linux

$ sudo yum remove app_name

$ sudo dnf remove app_name

When you want to update the applications:

$ yum update

$ sudo dnf upgrade – refresh

Uninstalling software from Linux system

You can install the software in the Linux system by using the repositories of the software. For viewing all the installed packages in the system you can use the command dpkg and then press Ctrl+Alt+T to open the terminal window. So, you can use the command like:

dpkg – list

You can scroll through the complete list of all the packages which have been installed in the system in the terminal window to find out what you want to uninstall from the system.

For uninstalling a package or program, you need to use the command apt-get which is the basic command for the purpose of installing as well as for

Kali Linux

manipulating all the programs which have been installed already. For instance, this command will be uninstalling gimp and will also delete all its configurations by using the -- purge command:

sudo apt-get -- purge remove gimp

You will need to enter your password here and then hit Enter. The process of uninstalling the program will start and the summary of the required actions which needs to be taken will be displayed on the screen. If you are asked if you want to continue with the process, type 'y' and then hit Enter. The process will continue. After the process is over, type 'exit' in the prompt and then hit Enter. It will close the terminal window. In case you do not want to wipe out the files of configuration, you will just need to leave out the -- purge command:

sudo apt-get remove gimp

When you are uninstalling any program, there might be other packages on which the uninstalled set of program was dependent. F
For removing any of the unused packages in the systems, you can use autoremove command:

sudo apt-get autoremove

Kali Linux

You can also combine two commands together for the purpose of removing any program along with its dependencies which are not used any longer by:

sudo apt-get purge – auto-remove gimp

In case you are running out of space in the system, use the command clean for removing all the downloaded files of archive:

sudo apt-get clean

This command will also be removing the cache in /var/cache/apt/archives.

So, installing and uninstalling software on Linux is a very easy and simple job using the command line.

Controlling Files and Directory Permissions

For most users of Linux, getting used to permissions and ownership of the files might be a bit challenging. It is assumed that for this usage level, using the command line is a must. Although there are several other more powerful and flexible options available, opting for the complicated commands is not always necessary. With help from some of the user-friendly interfaces of

Kali Linux

desktop, you can easily move to little or no usage of command line. It is possible to manage file ownership and permission as well.

The management of folders and files can be easily done from the inside of the file managers only. But, right before we get away with GUI, you will need to have a concrete understanding of what it is doing. So, let's start off with the command line.

Command line: File permissions

The commands associated with modification of file ownership and permissions are:

chmod: For changing the permissions

chown: For changing the ownership

Neither of the two commands is difficult to use. It is really important for you to understand that the sole user who can actually change the permissions or ownership of the files is the root user or the current owner. So, in case you are user B, you will not be able to make any changes to the folders and files which are owned by A without seeking help of the root or sudo. For instance:

Kali Linux

A new folder has been created on a partition of data known as /DATA/SHARE. Both users A and B require write as well as read permissions for this folder. There are various ways in which this can be achieved. If A and B are the only two users on the present system, you can easily change all the permissions of the files and folders for giving them access. You can do this with the command:

sudo chmod –R ugo+rw /DATA/SHARE

In this command, the breakdown of each and every command will be:

- sudo: This command is used for the purpose of gaining overall administrator rights for the command on any form of system which employs sudo.
- chmod: This command is used for modifying the permissions.
- -R: This command modifies all the permissions of the parent state of folder along with the child objects which are in it.
- ugo+rw: This command provides group, user and other write and read access.

  In this command, u stands for user, g for group and o for other. The o or other entry is the most dangerous of all as it will be giving permissions to everyone for the files and folders. The permissions which can be provided for a folder or file are:

Kali Linux

1. r: read
2. w: write
3. x: execute

The use of the switch –R is very important. In case you have various sub-files and folders within the directory SHARE and you want the permissions to get applied from the parent object to the following child objects, you have to use –R switch to make sure that the same permissions are being applied down to the deepest folder contained within the object of parent.

Command line: Ownership of file

Changing the file and folder ownership is also very easy and simple. Suppose A moved out a folder for B into the directory named SHARE but A still has the ownership. This whole thing can be modified by using a very simple command:

sudo chown –R B /DATA/SHARE

This whole command line can be broken down like:

- sudo: This command holds the administrator rights as you are dealing with a file or folder which is owned by another user.

Kali Linux

- chown: This command is used for changing the ownership.
- -R: This command acts as the recursive switch for making sure that all the child objects obtain the same changes of ownership.
- B: This is the new owner of the file/folder.
- /DATA/SHARE: This is the directory which is being modified.

GUI: Permissions for files

Suppose you need to allow everyone to gain permissions of write and read for the folder EXAMPLE. For doing this within the file manager of your Linux distribution, you are required to follow all the following steps:

- Open your Linux distribution.
- Navigate to the file or folder which is the target in this case.
- Right click on that folder or file.
- Click on Properties from the menu.
- Select the Permissions tab.
- Select the Access Files option in the Others tab.
- Click on Create and Delete Files.
- Select Change Permissions for the enclosed files.
- A window will pop up where you need to select Read and Write option under the tab of Files and Create and Delete Files under the Folders.
- Select Change.
- Click on Close.

Kali Linux

The trick comes into play when you need to modify the permissions for a folder which does not even belong to you. For doing this:

- Open up the terminal window.
- Enter the command: sudo –i.
- Enter the command: Nautilus.

The command sudo –i will give you a persistent form of access to sudo unless and until you enter the command Exit for removing the access. Once Nautilus is opened, you can easily modify the permissions for the folder or file, even if the file or folder does not belong to you.

GUI: Ownership modification

You can change the ownership for a file through Nautilus by following these steps:

- Locate the file or folder in the window of Nautilus.
- Right click on the file/folder.
- Select the Permissions tab.
- Click on New Owner from the drop-down menu of Owner.
- Select Close.

Kali Linux

Managing User Environment Variables

The most common area in which newcomers to Linux find hardest to manage the user environment variables might also be the most obscure of all. Although the environment of Windows comes with environment variables, most of the users manage their own variables. For getting the most out of Linux OS, you will need to understand as well as manage all the environment variables in the very first place for the optimal form of performance, convenience and stealth. The environment variables are the form of variables which are being used in the specific user environment. In majority of the cases, the environment will be the shell of BASH.

Every user along with the root comes with a specific set of environment variables which are all set at some default values until they are modified. You can easily change all these values for the purpose of making your system perform more efficiently and also customize your working environment.

Viewing the environment variables

You can start by viewing all the environment variables by simply entering 'env.' You will need to understand that all the available environment variables will be in upper case like PATH, SHELL, HOME, among many others. You can also create your own set of user-defined variables which will be discussed later. The command list will print out various variables which are unique to your system. In majority of the cases, this command list is so

Kali Linux

long that it cannot be viewed in one single page. For viewing all the variables arranged line by line, you can print out the output by using the command More.

After you have used the command More, the whole list of variables will be filled up on one screen and will stop. It will be waiting for you to hit the Enter key to advance to the next line. You can continue to do this until you have found any variable which you are looking out for. When you hit the Enter key a number of times, you will be finding out a variable known as HISTSIZE. When you again hit Enter, you will be taken through each and every variable of these, one after the other. When you are using the command More for viewing the output, you can enter q for quitting or exiting and then return to the prompt of command.

In place of just scrolling this long list of variables, a tedious job to look for the variable of your interest, you can also use the command 'grep' which acts as the filtering command and will help in easily finding out your required variable.

Viewing the values of the variables

The command 'set' will be displaying all the names of the variables, but if you want to view the values which are stored within the variables, you will need to

Kali Linux

enter the keyword 'echo' which needs to be followed by $ sign along with the name of the variable such as:

echo $HISTSIZE

The $ sign indicates that you want to function with the variable value which is available inside and not the label of the variable.

Exporting the environment variables

When you modify any environment variable, it is only for that specific set of environment. In this case, the environment is the BASH shell. This indicates that when you close the terminal, any of the modifications which you have made to these variables will be lost and will go back to their default value.

If you want the new variable values to stay for your next session of the terminal and the terminal session after that, you will need to export the variables. You can think of this as exporting the brand new variable value from the present variable to the remaining system to make sure it remains available in each and every environment. You can do this very easily by:

export HISTSIZE

Kali Linux

Now, the variable value of HISTSIZE is set to zero when you leave the environment. However, you can easily put the value of HISTSIZE back to what it was, suppose 1000 by entering:

HISTSIZE=1000

Export HISTSIZE

Changing the shell prompt

The shell prompt by default in Kali comes in the following format:

username@hostname:present_directory>

If you are the root user, it will translate the prompt:

root@kali:present_directory

You can also change the command prompt which by default is setting up the value for PS1 variable. This specific variable comes with a specific set of placeholders for all the information meant to be placed within the prompt. It includes:

\u: Name of the present user

\h: Name of the host

Kali Linux

\W: Present working directory

You can change the prompt in the terminal for PS1 by:

PSl= "Best Man:#"

Now, each and every time when you will open your terminal, it will show Best Man first.

You need to note that the prompt will be Best Man when you open up the first terminal which is PS1 but the second number of the terminal will still be the same which was set by default prompt.

Changing the PATH variable

The PATH variable is regarded as the most important of all. This variable ultimately controls the location to which your shell looks out for the commands which you type like 'ls,' 'cd,' 'echo' and many others. In case the shell of BASH is unable to find your command in any of the directories in any of your path, it will be returning an error message as "command not found". In case you want to install a completely new tool named "newtool" into the directory of /root/newtool, you can do this by adding it to the PATH variable by entering:

Kali Linux

PATH=$PATH:/root/newtool

Echo $PATH

The new tool will be added.

Kali Linux

Chapter 5: Real World Application of Kali Linux and Other Useful Tools

If you want to become an ethical hacker it will not be as easy as becoming a software developer of or a programmer. Ethical hackers, also known as penetration testers, need to have a proper understanding about various forms of fields.

Not only will you need in-depth knowledge about the various languages of programming such as in

C++, C and Python, you will also need advanced knowledge about the Linux environment to get started with ethical hacking.

Kali Linux is a distribution of Linux which comes with around 600 pre-installed tools which are meant for penetration testing. As a beginner in the world of penetration testing, this might sound irritating. How could someone learn to use all 600 tools as a beginner? However, the truth behind all these tools is that you don't need to master all the tools. This is mainly because Kali Linux comes with various tools which serve the same purpose and concept. Let's have a look at some of the best tools that Kali Linux offers for the purpose of ethical hacking.

MacChanger

MAC address can be regarded as the legal address of any system. There are various reasons why it is important to change your MAC address.

Kali Linux

MacChanger helps in changing the MAC address at the time of penetration testing such pentesting any wireless form of network with filtering of MAC enabled. For using the MacChanger , you will need to follow this command:

~$ macchanger [options] networkDevice

The options which are available are:

-h, -- help: Prints help

-V, -- version: Prints the version and then exits

-e, --ending: Do not change the bytes of vendor

-s, --show: Prints the MAC address and then exits

-a, --another: Sets up random vendor MAC which is of the similar kind

-p, --permanent: Resets to the original form of permanent hardware MAC

-A: Sets up random vendor MAC which is of any kind

-r, --random: Sets up absolutely random type of MAC address

-l, --list: Prints the vendors which are known

-m, --mac=XX:XX:XX:XX:XX:XX: Sets the MAC address as XX:XX:XX:XX:XX:XX

Nmap

This works as a network mapping tool. It allows the user to find out the active form of hosts within any network and then gather all form of information

Kali Linux

relevant to the task of penetration testing. The main features of this tool are:

- It helps in host discovery. It can easily identify the hosts in a network.
- It comes with the feature of port scanning. It allows you to enumerate all the open form of ports on the remote or local host.
- It helps in gathering information related to the operating system along with hardware about any form of device which is connected.
- It also helps in determining the name and version of any application.
- It extends the default capabilities of Nmap by utilizing the Nmap Scripting Engine or NSE.

Netcat

This is a network exploration tool which is famous in the world of security and well known in the fields of system and network administration. It is primarily used for checking of inbound and outbound network along with exploration of port. It is also helpful when used together with other programming languages such as C or Perl or along with scripting of BASH. The main features of this tool are:

- It performs analysis of TCP and UDP ports.
- It performs sniffing of inbound as well outbound network.
- It helps in reverse and forward analysis of DNS.

Kali Linux

- It performs scanning of remote and local ports.
- It comes fully integrated with the standard terminal input.
- It comes with TCP and UDP tunneling mode.

Unicornscan

This is a type of infosec tool used for gathering of information and correlation of data. It comes with asynchronous scanning of UDP and TCP ports along with the feature of finding out network patterns which can help in finding out the remote form of hosts. It can also provide details about all software which are being run by them. The main features of this tool are:

- It performs asynchronous scan of TCP port.
- It performs asynchronous scan of UDP port.
- It performs asynchronous detection of TCP banner.
- It can detect OS system service along with application status.
- It comes with the ability to use custom sets of data.
- It also supports relational output for SQL.

Fierce

It is a tool used for mapping of network and scanning of ports. It can also be used for discovering the non-contiguous space of IP along with the hostnames across various networks. It is somewhat similar to that of Unicornscan and Nmap but unlike these two, Fierce is specifically being used for corporate networks. After the penetration tester defines the target

Kali Linux

network, this tool runs various tests against the domains which have been selected for retrieving information which can be used for analysis in later stage and for exploitation. The main features of this tool include:

- It comes with the ability to change the DNS server for the purpose of reverse lookups.
- It performs internal as well as external IP range scanning.
- It performs scanning of IP range as well as of complete Class C.
- It helps in logging the capabilities into a file system.
- It discovers the name servers and also finds out the zone transfer attack.
- It comes with capabilities of brute force by using the custom or built-in list of texts.

There are various other tools from Linux which help in penetration testing as well as for ethical hacking . Each of the tools come with its own set of usability and can be used easily by any penetration tester.

Chapter 6: Programming Linux

Programming on Linux is used for creating interfaces, applications, software and programs. Linux code is often used for the desktop, embedded systems as well as for real-time programs. Linux is an open source OS kernel which is compatible with Perl, C++, Java and various other languages of programming.

How does Linux work?

Linux functions as the kernel of an OS which can also be distributed and shared freely. An operating system or OS is that interface which helps in connecting the users with the hardware of the computer and also supports the running of the applications and programs. Kernel is nothing but the OS core as it manages all the communication between the components of hardware and software.

What are the functions of the Linux programmers?

Starting off with Linux programming employs tools such as GBU compiler and debugger. They help in creating applications for the storage of data, construction of GUI and also script writing. More advanced applications related to Linux allow the programmers to develop software related to Linux. They also optimize the programs which are already existing and also write new programs with various complex form of features such as

Kali Linux

multiprocessing, multi-threading, inter-process communication and also interaction of hardware device.

Uses of Linux

Linux is widely used today in various servers, computer security systems and architecture of computer system. It is widely used in real-time programs along with the embedded systems of PDAs and cell phones. Linux programming has also resulted in various applications.

How to develop the modules of Kernel?

Before you start off with core programming in Linux, the best way of increasing your knowledge along with expertise of Linux programming is to start working on the kernel module. The modules are developed independently which works with the Linux kernels for functioning as a compact operating system. The kernel modules consist of various things such as drivers of devices for the several peripheries of hardware, file managers and other low-level features of the OS.

The only barrier that comes at the entry of kernel module is much lower in rate than there are for working on the kernel of Linux. There are several modules which are being developed by various individuals and teams. So, there is no specific gatekeeper at the entry of development.

Logical Breakdown of Programming in Linux

Kali Linux

When you are using some of the major forms of operating system then you are interacting indirectly to the shell. If you are using Linux Mint, Ubuntu or any other proper distribution of Linux, you will be interacting with the shell every single time you will use the terminal. Let us discuss the breakdown of programming in Linux which consists of Linux shells along with scripting of shell.

So, before we start, you will need to get acquainted with some of these terminologies:

- Kernel
- Shell
- Terminal

What is a kernel?

Kernel is nothing but a program which acts as the core of the operating system. It comes with overall control over all the elements in a system. It helps in managing various resources of the systems based on Linux:

- Management of files
- Management of processes
- Management of I/O
- Management of memory

Kali Linux

- Management of the devices and various other components

A complete system of Linux can be broken down like: Kernel + installation scripts + other scripts of management + GNU system libraries and utilities.

What is a shell?

A shell is a special type of user program which helps in providing a proper interface to the services related to an operating system. The shells accept commands which are readable by humans from the users and then converts those into something which can be understood by the kernel. It can be regarded as the interpreter of command language which helps in executing the commands which are read from the devices of input like the keyboard or from the files in the system. A shell starts when a user logs into the system or starts with a terminal.

A shell can be easily classified into two different categories:
- Graphical shell
- Command line shell

The graphical shells provide various means for the purpose of manipulating the programs which are based on the GUI or graphical user interface. This is done by letting the operations like closing, opening, resizing and moving windows, along with switching the focus in between the windows. Ubuntu OS

Kali Linux

along with Windows OS can be regarded as great examples which provide the GUI to the users for the purpose of interacting with various programs.

Shells can be accessed by users by using the CLI or command line interface. A special type of program in Linux known as the terminal is provided for typing in the commands of the humans like ls, cat and many others and further which are being executed. The final result is then displayed directly on the terminal which can be seen by the user. Suppose you execute the command ls along with the option –l. This will be listing all the available files within the present working directory in a form of long listing.

Working along with the command line shell might turn out to be a bit difficult if you are a beginner only because of the fact that it is tough to memorize a bunch of commands at the same time. It is highly powerful in nature and it also allows the users to store all the commands within a specific file and then execute all of them together. In this way, any form of repetitive task can easily be made automatic. All of these files are generally known as Shell Scripts in the Linux systems.

In a Linux system, there are various types of shells which are available for the users:

- BASH: Also known as Bourne Again Shell, it is widely used in the systems which are based on Linux. It is being used as the default shell of login in the Linux systems. If you want, you can also install this in the Windows operating system.

- CSH: Also known as the C shell, it uses the syntax of the C shell and its usage is more or less similar to the programming language of C.
- KSH: Also known as the Korn shell, it is the base of the POSIX Shell standard.

Each of the shells functions in the same way but all of them understand various commands and also provides various built-in functions.

Scripting of Shell

In general, the shells are interactive in nature which means that they can accept the commands as inputs from the users and can also execute them. However, it might happen that you need to or want to execute a whole bunch of commands in a routine manner, so you will need to type all the commands every time within the terminal. As the shells can also take in the commands in the form of inputs from the files, you can also write the commands within a file and then execute them in the shell for avoiding the task of repetition. All of these files are known as Shell Programs or Shell Scripts. The shell scripts are somewhat similar in structure with the batch file which can be found in MS-DOS. Each of the shell scripts is saved with the extension of .sh file such as yourscript.sh.

Kali Linux

The shell scripts also come with syntax like all other languages of programming. In case you are already acquainted with any programming languages like C, C++ or Python, it will be easier for you to start with shell scripting. The shell scripts consist of:

- Shell Keywords: It includes else, if, break and many others
- Shell Commands: It includes ls, cd, echo, touch, pwd and many others
- Control Flow: It includes if..then..else, shell and case loops and many others

You can use shell scripts for avoiding the repetitive work and thus opting for automation. It also helps in monitoring of the system, and allows the addition of various new functionalities to the shells.

Programming in Linux Using C

Linux is turning out to be a heaven of programming for developers. It is mainly because of the open source nature of Linux and also being a completely free operating system. Turbo C compiler is the old form of compiler which has been used for compiling programs. The same job can be done on Linux for creating a new environment of programming. Let's have a

Kali Linux

look at how to get started with programming in Linux by using C for writing, compiling and running programs based on C.

If you have not yet installed any Linux distribution on your system such as Ubuntu, you can do it by installing any virtual machine on the system like the VirtualBox. It is a product which has been designed by Oracle to allow the users to run any form of virtual machine on the computer system. This means that you can easily run Linux on your Apple or Windows system. After you have downloaded your virtual machine, install it on your computer and then restart your system and then create a brand new virtual machine. For creating a virtual machine:

- Press the New button for creating new VM.
- Provide a proper name to your virtual machine.
- Select the operating system as Linux and Ubuntu 64 bit.
- Click on Next.
- Click on Create Virtual Hard Disk.
- Click on Create.

How to install C language on Linux?

Kali Linux

- Open up the terminal window. For this go to Applications then Accessories and then click on Terminal. This will open up a new terminal window.
- For the purpose of running C program in the system, you will need to install the essential packages. For achieving this, you will need to enter the command in the terminal window as:

  sudo apt-get install build-essential

  It will now ask for the administrator password. After you have entered the password correctly, the process of installation will begin. For the purpose of installing the packages, you will need to be connected with the Internet. It will take some time to complete which will depend on the speed of the internet.
- Now you can write and run your desired program.

How to write programs based on C in Linux?

For writing C program in Linux follow these steps:

- Open up any text editor such as gedit. You can do this by entering the command gedit prog.c.
- Write the program. For instance: #include<stdio.h>int main(){ printf("Hello"); return 0;}
- Then save the program with .c extension.
- Then you will need to compile the program.
- Then you can run or execute the program.

Kali Linux

Programming in depth

- Enter the command mentioned below in the terminal window to open up a text editor.

  gedit prog.c

- After the text editor has opened up, you can now write the program.
- After you are done with writing your program, save it and then close the text editor.
- You can compile the program as below:

  gcc prog.c –o prog

- If there is no error within your written program, nothing will be shown on the screen. If there is any form of error in your program it will be shown. You will also need to open up the text editor again and then repeat all the steps for removing the error and then save it.
- For running the program enter this command:

  ./prog

- After the program has run, you can see the program output in another terminal window.

Kali Linux

Programming in Linux using C++

C can be regarded as a language of programming which is of procedural nature. It was developed between 1969 and 1973 by Dennis Ritchie. Initially, it was developed as a programming language for the purpose of writing up a complete operating system. The main features of the C++ language come with low-level accessing of system memory, a very simple and easy set of keywords and a very clean style. All these features make the C++ language very much suitable for all sort of system programming such as operating system or even development of a compiler. The first step includes installation of some development tools along with several applications like GCC, GNU, C++ compiler for the task of compiling the program and for executing the overall code in Linux. C and C++ are somewhat similar and for understanding C++ let us first have a look at C.

If you want you can also verify the installed set of tools by using the command:

cc –v.

Let us now consider a very easy C program file which is named as Sort.c:

int main(void)
{

Kali Linux

 printf("Hello! Sort\n");

return 0;

}

For compiling this easy program you can use:

cc filename.c -o executable_file_name

In this command, the filename.c is the C program file and -o option has been used for showing up the errors in the code. If there is no error in the code, it will generate an executable form of file named as executable_file_name.

cc Sort.c -o sortoutput

In this, sortoutput is the file which is executable in nature and it is being generated. So, you can execute the same like:

./sortoutput

For program files related to C++

C++ is a programming language which has been developed for the general purpose of programming and is being widely used today for competitive programming.

It comes with object-oriented, imperative and generic program features. You can run C++ on various OS platforms such as Linux, Windows, Mac, Unix and many others. Before we start programming by using C++, you will need a proper environment which needs to be set up on your computer system for

Kali Linux

the purpose of compiling and running your C++ based programs. You can verify all your installed tools on C++ by using this command:

g++ -- version

Let us consider a very simple C++ program:

// main function

// where the execution

// of program starts

int main()

{

// print Hello Universe!

cout<< "Hello Universe!\n";

return 0;

}

For compiling this entire code you can use:

g++ filename.cpp -o executable_file_name

Here in this command, filename.cpp is the file of C++ program and -o option has been used for showing out the errors within the code. In case no error has been found, it will generate an executable form of file named as executable_file_name.

g++ sort.cpp -o sortoutput

Here in this command, sortoutput is the executable form of file which is being generated. So, you can execute the same such as:

./sortoutput

Kali Linux

Installing compiler for C++ in Linux

If you are using a Linux based system such as CentOS, Red Hat, Fedora or something else, you can type in this command as the root for installing the compiler of C++:

yum install –y gcc-c++*

In order to verify that the compiler of GCC has been installed properly in the system use:

rpm –qa | grep –i c++

You can also use the which command as:

which c++

Writing the first C++ based program on Linux

- From the terminal window, open up a new file for the purpose of editing by using the command vim as:

  vim hello.cc

- Within the vim editor, you can now type your C++ program or code.
- After you are done, save and then exit the file.
- For compiling the new program of C++, you will need to type this command in the terminal:

  c++ hello.cc

  If the compilation process runs without any error, no form of output is going to be printed on the screen.

Kali Linux

- An executable form of file will be created within the present directory with a.out as the default name.
- For running this same program, you can execute the executable file which has been generated in a similar way you execute any of the executables of Linux.

How to specify name meant for the executable which has been generated?

Compiling the programs of C++ without any of the specifying options will be producing an executable form of file with the name a.out. If you want to specify a particular name for the executable of your choice you have two ways: first, is to rename the a.out default after it has been created and second, is to specify the filename of the executable at the time of compilation by using the option –o.

c++ hello.cc –o /opt/hello.run

Executing the system commands from programs of C++

It is very important to be able to communicate with the compiling system by executing the commands of OS when needed. The system() function will allow you to run the commands of the system from the code of C++. For the ease of the compiler to recognize all these functions properly and for compiling in the proper way, stdlib.h library file is required to be invoked.

Kali Linux

Bottom line

- For writing down C or C++ based programs on the machines based on Linux, you will need the GCC compiler.
- All the C++ programs are saved and written as .cc format of files.
- All the resulting form of executables can also be executed in a similar way the Linux or Unix executables are being executed.
- The system function is used for running commands of the system from the code of C++.
- The g++ and c++ command both compile and link with the source files of C++.

Programming in Linux Using Python

Python is one of the modern-day programming languages which has been gaining lots of traction in the development community. It was developed by Guido von Rossum in 1990. It is somewhat like Java in which the programs, once written can be easily run on any type of operating system. If you are starting off with programming for the first time in Linux, Python is a great choice for you to begin with. It comes with a low learning curve along with an elegant system of coding.

Kali Linux

Installation of Python

Linux based distributions such as Ubuntu come with a version of command line pre-installed which makes the ultimate game of starting with Python very easy and simple. In fact, many in the Linux community developed many of the scripts and sets of tools under Python.

You can start the process with either the graphical interactive development environment or IDLE or command line version.

Programming Python from the command line

Open up your terminal window and then type in python within quotes as 'python'. This will open up Python in the interactive mode. This mode is really good for learning at the initial stages, however, you might want to use a text editor such as Vim, Gedit or Emacs for writing down your codes. As long as you save the codes with the extension of .py, you can execute them in the terminal window. Most of the programming starts with the very old standby: the program of Hello Universe or World. So, we will also start it from there.

At the command prompt, type in print "Hello Universe" and then hit enter. You can readily see the command being printed on the line next to the command. For running a script from the command line just type: python my_script.py. If you want to exit from the command line type in exit () or just hit Ctrl+d.

Kali Linux

Programming Python with IDLE

If you are thinking of writing down a long program right from the command line, you can start with IDLE. Just open up the terminal window and then type in: 'idle'. You will now see that the graphical shell of Python has been loaded. For writing down a script in Python, just click on File then New Window.

This will be opening up a kind of text editor just like Notepad. Then, all you need to do is to just type this code:

#linuxversion.py

#Have user input version and response

name= raw_input("Which release of Linux do you see")

print "Even I like", name, " – Linux is great!"

A variety of things are going on here in this command. The first two lines which are preceded by the sign # are just mere comments. The third line will be using the input which has been gathered from the function raw_input and then it will assign the same to a variable which is a name.

At the end, the print statement will return the results. You can save the file with an extension of .py and then select Run followed by Run Module from the available menu for running your program.

Kali Linux

Note that there are various programming languages which generally ignore any of the whitespaces which is actually the spacing in between the codes. However, in the case of Python, when there is any form of improper spacing it can lead to syntax errors. So, make sure that you enter the spaces properly for running the code properly.

Python Programming

It is often said that systems administrators are required to be very proficient with the language of scripting.

While most of the people are very much comfortable in using BASH for running the scripts, Python in place of it can actually add several benefits. Python allows the users to access all the tools of the command line and also makes use of the Object Oriented Programming structure. The versions of Python: 2.x and 3.x can be usually found for most of the distributions of Linux. For entering a shell of Python just type in python3 or python in the emulator of your terminal. For exiting from the shell just type in quit().

It is to be noted that while version 2.x of Python is still used today, it is not at all maintained actively. For this reason, it is always better to switch to 3.x. There are certain differences in syntax in both the versions of Python.

You can perform various arithmetic operations along with manipulation of text strings in Python. If you want you can even assign the operational results to the variables and then display the same on the screen. A very handy feature that comes with Python is concatenation: you will need to supply the variable or string values in a list which is comma-delimited for printing the function and it will return the sentence completely composed by the listed items in a sequence. You can also mix up variables of various types and after you have assigned one specific value to any of the variables, you can change the type of data in a later stage without any form of problem.

You can easily create lists in Python. A list is nothing but an ordered set of items which is not at all necessary to be of the similar data type. For creating an empty set of list names as bandsRock, you will need to use square brackets along with the command as:

bandsRock=[]

For appending any of the items to the bottom of the list use append(). For removing any of the items from the list, you can easily pass the particular element to the method remove() or the proper position of the item in the list as pop(). For displaying the complete list of the available methods for any object you can use Ctrl+space after you have typed in the item name along with a dot.

Kali Linux

Programming in Linux Using Java

Java is one of the most popular languages of programming. It is widely used for the purpose of developing software for almost everything starting from cell phones to the cable TV boxes and extending its use to the large systems of enterprise information. The overall concept behind writing the source code of Java, compiling and then running it is more or less the same across most of the OS.

Java is a programming language which was originally developed by Sun Microsystems. It falls under the category of compiled form of programming language in which the programmer writes up the source code and then submits the same to the compiler which will be checking out the syntaxes of the program and will generate a complete file which you can run. For instance, when you are using Google Chrome web browser, you are in true sense running all the programs which have been generated from a compiler which is used by the software developers.

To a wide extent, the programming languages of the past needed you to re-compile all the source code for every new OS in which you wanted to run your program on. For instance, a program which has been compiled for running in Windows will not be running on a system which has Linux in it unless it has been re-compiled. Given the wide differences in the OS and the elements of

Kali Linux

hardware, this process was very difficult and complicated to carry out. One of the major motivations for Java was the motivation of being able to write only one single set of source code and then provide the resulting program with the ability to run on some different set of operating systems or environments of operation.

Java comes with write once and then run anywhere capability only because of the way in which the compiler translates the entire source code in a particular file known as Byte Code file which can then run under any form of supported JRE or Java Runtime Environment.

The development process of Java involves these steps:

- Write down the Java source code and then save it in one or more plain text files. All of these files generally come with .java format at the end.
- Run the compiler of Java (javac) for compiling the source code which you have written into a file of Byte Code. The Byte Codes generally have .class at the end of the name of the file.
- Run the program after submitting the byte code to a JRE.

Kali Linux

Downloading Java Development Kit

For doing any of the programming stuff with Java, you will need to download, and then install, Java Development Kit or JDE. In most cases, when you come across the installation of Java in a system it means the installation of Java Runtime Environment or JRE. In this example, you will need JDK which comes with a special type of program named as javac which is used for compiling the Java source codes into the class files. You can download JDK from the official website of Oracle.

While downloading the JDK, make sure that you download the one which matches with the operating system that you are currently using. In this case, if you are using Linux, download the file which is supported by Linux OS. Most of the distributions of Linux like Ubuntu, Debian, Red Hat and others, come with a tool of software repository which helps in automating the installation along with the download steps. For instance, under the distribution of Ubuntu and Debian, the command apt-get is used for downloading and then installing JDK such as:

sudo apt-get install openjdk-7-jdk

For installing the OpenJDK under Fedora, CentOS and other distributions which use up YUM, you can use this command:

Kali Linux

yum install java-1.7.0-openjdk

Both the apt-get as well as yum installers will be downloading, installing and then configuring the JDK without any form of additional task on the part of the user.

Writing and compiling Java program

The programming language of Java is a form of compiled language in which the programmer writes up the source code and it is then submitted to the compiler. A compiler is nothing but a program which helps in converting source code into Byte Code.

The Byte Code which comes out as a result is executed with the use of the JRE. You can write the source code of Java by the use of any text editor, like Notepad in Windows and in Linux pico or nano editors which are used for editing the files of source code. For starting off with Java program follow these steps:

- Open up shell prompt in Linux. You can also achieve this by pressing ALT+Ctrl+T in Linux.
- Create a new file by using the program gedit by simply typing:
  gedit HelloUniverse.java
  The gedit program will open up and will create a file.
- Type in your Java source code.

Kali Linux

- After you are done with your source code, make sure that you save it.
- Exit from the gedit program.
- Now it's the time to compile the program with the use of javac compiler. The command will be: javac HelloUniverse.java
- If there is no error in the syntax, the compiler will run smoothly.
- Now you can run the sample program which you have created by running Java and then followed by the program name.

Java programming also includes another component known as the class. It is a large collection of functions which carries out various work along with templates for the various data which might be carried on. In the program example which was mentioned just before this, HelloUniverse is the class of the program.

Scripting on Linux Using BASH

BASH is an interpreter of command language. It is available widely on various types of operating systems and it also acts as the default interpreter of command for most of the Linux or GNU systems. BASH works with shells. A shell is nothing but a macro processor which lets non-interactive or interactive form of command execution. In BASH, scripting allows execution of automatic commands which would have been otherwise executed one by one in an interactive form.

Basics of Bash Shell

A shell allows the user to interact with the computer by using the commands. It also helps in storing and retrieving data, processing of information and several other tasks. For example, you can type in commands such as cal, date, pwd or ls and then hit the Enter key. What you have just done is interacted with the system by the use of the shell to retrieve the present date and time.

It was done by using date, checking out the calendar by using cal, checking out the location of your present directory on which you are working by using pwd and then retrieving a complete list of directories and files which is located within ls.

What is meant by scripting?

For understanding scripting in the proper way, first use the shell in combination with the text editor that you use such as .vi for creating a brand new file named as task.sh which will contain all the commands from above, each of the commands on different lines. After you are done with this, you will need to make the new file completely executable by using the command

Kali Linux

chmod along with an option +x. Lastly, all that you need is to execute the new script by prefixing the name along with ./.

By the use of proper scripting, any form of shell interaction can be scripted as well as automated. It is also possible now to execute the new shell script task.sh automatically daily at any time you want by using cron time-based scheduler and then store the output of the script to a specific file every time it is executed.

Basics of BASH

Till now we have discussed shell and scripting. But, what about BASH? As we have already discussed earlier, BASH is a default form of interpreter for many Linux or GNU based systems. That is the reason why our last shell script worked even without the definition of bash as the final interpreter.

For finding out what is the interpreter by default you can execute this command:

$ echo $SHELL

/bin/bash

You can also find out several other interpreters of shell, like C shell, Korn shell and various others. To define the script interpreter as BASH, you will need to locate first a complete path for its executable binary by using the command 'which'. This command needs to be prefixed with shebang or # !. You will need to insert this at the very first line of the script. There are other methods for defining your shell interpreter, but this is regarded as the best option.

File permissions and names

In order to execute the shell script, your file needs to be in executable form by using the command chmod +x FILENAME. Any form of newly created files will not be in the executable form by default, regardless of the suffix of the file extension. On the systems based on Linux or GNU the command 'file' is used for identifying the file type.

Execution of script

In simple terms, a bash script is nothing but a simple text file which contains instructions which need to be executed in proper order from the top to the bottom. The way in which the instructions are interpreted depends on the defined shebang or the process in which the script is being executed.

There is another method of executing the bash scripts in which the bash interpreter is called in explicit order such as by $ bash date.sh. By calling out the binary executable in explicit form, the file content of date.sh is being loaded up and then interpreted as the bash shell script.

Kali Linux

Simple Backup Shell Script

Any of the commands which can be executed successfully via the bash shell terminal can be in the similar form which is being used as a part of the shell script of bash. There is no proper differentiation between the direct execution of

command through the terminal or within a script of shell away from the fact that script shell offers a non-interactive form of execution for the various commands within a single process. Most of the commands accept arguments and options. The command options are being used for modifying the behavior of the commands for the purpose of producing alternative form of output results which are prefixed by -. The arguments can specify the execution of commands for the target like directory, file, text and others.

You can use the command 'man' for displaying the manual page of any of the desired command. For instance, in order to display the manual page for the command ls you can execute the command man ls. For quitting the manual page you can press the key 'q'.

Variables

Variables can be regarded as the prime essence of programming. This allows the programmers to store up the data, reuse and then alter the same throughout the complete script. You can create a brand new script such as welcome.sh by using variables.

Kali Linux

Input and Output

The commands which are executed on the Linux/GNU command line either require input, produce the output or display an error message. This is a very basic concept of shell scripting along with working with the command line of Linux or GNU in general.

The commands which are executed on the Linux/GNU command line either require input, produce the output or display an error message. This is a very basic concept of shell scripting along with working with the command line of Linux or GNU in general. Each time you execute a command, there are three possible outcomes: The first possibility is it will be producing an output, the second possibility will be generating an error and the third possibility might not produce any form of output.

Kali Linux

Chapter 7: Basics of Networking

In today's world where everything comes with the touch of technology, networking has turned out to be a mandatory component for setting up a new business or organization. Networking helps in seamlessly connecting with a set of related devices or systems with the endpoints or rather the host or master system via various forms. It holds a very important position for all providers of services, businesses and the consumers all around the globe to communicate and interconnect with each other at the same time.

The concept of networking comes along with almost everything such as text messages, calling on the telephone, streaming of video and many more.

The operation of networks comes along with some serious set of skills which largely depends on its complexity. For example, in a large enterprise where there are several nodes along with requirements of network security such as functioning of the administrator, encryption and various others. On the other hand, any person who just uses networking along with the internet for day to day work at home can set up easily along with troubleshooting of the several problems of basic nature within the nature of wireless networks.

Networking basics

For properly understanding the functioning of networking along with its components, you will need to know about the basics. A network of computer systems is built up of several elements which help in the overall functioning.

Kali Linux

Types of networking

Networking of computers can be classified into two main categories: wired and wireless. While talking about a wired network, it requires a physical form of network which is needed for the transportation of information between the two nodes. For digital communication in business places and homes, Ethernet cables are being used owing to their overall cost-effectiveness along with durability. Today, optical fibers are also being used for transportation of data across long distances.

Optical fibers also offer a faster rate of speed than Ethernet cables. However, Ethernet cables are much cheaper when compared with optical fibers.

In a wireless form of networking, radio waves are utilized for data transportation through the air. In this, the devices are connected to one another without any type of cables in between them. Wireless LAN is being used most widely for the purpose of wireless networking. There are various alternatives which can be found today like Bluetooth, satellite, cellular, microwave and various others.

After various practical experiences, it has been found that the wired form of networking comes with much better speed and security plus reliability as compared with the wireless mode of networking. But, with wireless networking comes greater probability of scalability, mobility and flexibility than the wired form of networking. Both types of networking are being classified in accordance with the physical layer of the networks. It can also be differentiated according to the build and design structure of the networks, network overlay and approaches which are made for encompassing SDN. The networks can also be categorized by the scale, WAN, LAN, network storage area, environment and various other aspects.

Networking system and its types

When you come across networking systems you will find two different types: open and closed. Within an open system, the whole system stays connected with the network which is ready for any type of communication. In a closed system, the system stays unlinked with the network and you will not be able to connect with the network.

Components of networking

The system of networking requires the infrastructure of a proper physical form of network. It consists of several networking components like switches, routers, access points and also some basic form of firmware which ultimately helps in the operation of the other connected components.

The other components include the software which is needed for the purpose of security, monitoring and management of the network. Any type of network depends largely on the protocols plus its standards for the performance of discrete form of jobs or for the purpose of communication with various data types. By protocol, it means a proper set of algorithms or set of rules which

Kali Linux

defines the ways in which the different entities related to communication connect with one another across a network. You can fund several types of protocols within a network like ARP, IP, TCP, FTP, DHCP and various others.

Voice over IP or VoIP is being used for the purpose of transporting the IP telephonic traffic directly to the final point which is also supported by the protocol. TCP/IP is regarded as the internet protocol suite which is responsible for the transportation of data across a network based on IP. An IP address can be regarded as the logical form of address which behaves as the address of the network for all the systems in a network. It provides help in setting up a unique form of identification for each and every device within a network. The IP addresses which are found for the network are in 32 bits structure. IPV4 is being assigned by the IANA for all the systems within a network.

The physical form of address of each and every network host is known as the MAC address. It stays linked with the network interface card or NIC. You can find MAC addresses in 48 bits or 12 nibble. The MAC addresses are assigned to the devices at the time of manufacturing.

Chapter 8: Proxies and Proxy Chains

With advances in technology, the number of hackers is also increasing day by day. While talking about hackers, some are good and some can be regarded as evil. Most of the evil hackers use the methods of hacking for stealing valuable and confidential information, for money or some even hack just for fun. The evil hackers have the tendency to create a situation of havoc in the world of cyber security by spreading harmful malware and other malicious items. The good hackers might also hack for money. But they do it the proper way like taking part in a bug bounty, by helping others to properly backup all With advances in technology, the number of hackers is also increasing day by day. While talking about of their lost data, learning the possible vulnerabilities within a system to make the administrators aware of the possible threats, among others.

By "hacker," it does not mean that they are the ones who can break into any form of restricted area within the world of cyber security; they are also IT experts who manage the security of a company or an organization. Most of the hackers are required to be anonymous at the time of hacking and they always try hard to make it difficult to detect them. There are various types of tools which are used by the hackers for hiding their identities such as VPN or Virtual Private Network, RDP or Remote Desktop Protocol and ProxyServers.

Kali Linux

To perform a penetration test absolutely anonymously and to decrease the overall chances of detection, hackers are required to use some kind of intermediary machinery whose very own IP address will be left back on the system of the target. The hackers fulfill this motive by the use of proxy. A proxy server or proxy is a form of dedicated system of software or computer which also runs on a computer system and acts as the intermediary between a client's server and the end device like a computer system. By connecting with the Internet via the proxies, the IP address of the client system will not be displayed but the IP address of the proxy server will be shown in place of it. It helps in providing the clients with an increased amount of privacy when they connect directly with the internet.

The features of ProxyChains

The primary features of ProxyChains are:

- It supports SOCKS4, SOCKS5 along with HTTP CONNECT based proxy servers.
- The ProxyChains can be mixed up with any other type of proxy in the list.
- ProxyChains does support various methods of chaining such as: random in which any random proxy within the list which is stored within a file of configuration or chaining proxies in the similar list of

order, the various form of proxies are kept separated from each other by the use of new line in the file. It also comes with a dynamic option in which the ProxyChains pass through only those proxies which are live in nature. It excludes any form of unreachable or dead proxy. This form of proxy is also known as the smart option.

- You can use the ProxyChains with servers such as sendmail, squid and many others.
- The ProxyChains also come with the ability of resolving DNS via the proxies.
- It can handle any form of TCP client application which is telnet, nmap and others.

Syntax of ProxyChains

In place of just running a simple penetration test or by creating various target requests directly by using your IP address, you can use ProxyChains for covering up and handling all these jobs. You will just need to add a command 'proxychains' for every job. This will enable the service of ProxyChains.

For instance, you want to scan some of the available hosts along with its ports in the network by the use of Nmap with ProxyChains, the command will look like:

proxychains nmap 192.168.0.0/25

The breakup of this command syntax will be:

Kali Linux

proxychains: This will tell the machine to run the service of ProxyChains nmap: Tells the ProxyChains about which jobs to be performed 192.168.0.0/25 or some other argument: It is the argument which is needed for any form of tool or job and in this case, it is your scan range which is needed for Nmap to run the scan.

How can ProxyChains be used?

Before you start to use ProxyChains, you will need to set up the configuration file for ProxyChains. You will also be requiring a list of the proxy servers. The configuration file of ProxyChains is located on /etc/proxychains.conf. Open up the file proxychains.conf in any text editor of your choice and then set up the overall configuration. By default settings, the proxychains will be directly sending the overall traffic first via your host at 127.0.0.1 on the port 9050 which is the default configuration for Tor. In case you are also using Tor, you can leave this whole thing as it is. If you are not using Tor, you will be required to comment this line out.

You will now need to add some more proxies. There are various free proxy servers that can be found on the Internet. Comment the proxy which is set by default for Tor. If you are not using it, then add the proxy on the config file of Proxychains and then save it.

Kali Linux

Random_Chain VS Dynamic_Chain

A Random Chain will allow you to choose the IP addresses in a random way from the list. Every time you use ProxyChains, the chain of the proxy will be looking different to the target and thus making it more difficult to track down the traffic from the source.

In Dynamic Chain, you can run your traffic via every proxy on the list and in case any of the proxies is not responding or is down, the dead proxies are completely skipped out and it will automatically go for the next proxy in line without giving an error message. Each of the connections is done through the chained proxies. Each and every proxy on the list is chained in an order as they appear in that list.

Chapter 9: Virtual Private Networks

Virtual Private Network or VPN is one of the latest techniques of setting up a super secure form of connection along with another form of network directly over the internet. VPNs are being widely used today for the sole purpose of accessing various websites which are restricted in various regions, for protecting all the activities of browsing from the prying eyes of public Wi-Fi and many others. Today, VPNs are widely popular but in most cases, it is not being used for the purpose for which it was developed. It was designed for connecting with the business network in a much more safe and secure way over the Web.

It also came on the market with the objective of allowing the users to access their business networks from their home only. This technique functions by forwarding all forms of traffic within a network by providing several benefits like accessing of local network resources remotely, bypassing any form of censorship on the web in some places, etc. Many of the operating systems which can be found today in the market also come with VPN pre-installed.

Benefits of using VPN

The concept on which VPN works is very easy and simple. It works by connecting a user directly with some other computer system or server over the internet. It then lets the user surf the contents available on the internet by

Kali Linux

bypassing and using the internet connection of that same server or computer. So, what makes VPN much more interesting is that if you have connected with a computer from some other province or country, it will show that you are also from that same country. So, you will be now able to access anything by using VPN along with those things which you couldn't have done normally.

You can use a VPN for a wide collection of purposes:

- You can use VPN for the purpose of bypassing any restriction on any website which is based on province or geography. You can also use VPN streaming of audio and video.
- You can watch any form of online streaming such as Netflix, Hulu etc.
- You can protect yourself from the radars at the time of accessing torrents.
- You can protect yourself from connecting to any type of harmful Wi-Fi hotspot .
- You can gain a greater amount of privacy while online by simply hiding the actual location of your system.

Majority of the users of VPN use this technique for bypassing the restrictions on their geography to access the contents which are restricted by using a network of some other province. It is also used for accessing and downloading content via torrent. However, VPNs can be really helpful at the time of accessing any form of public Wi-Fi such as the ones available in railway stations or coffee shops.

How can you get a VPN?

The VPN that you need will depend completely on your usage and requirements. You can start by either creating a VPN server for yourself or out of your house. In case you want to create a VPN from work you can do that as well. In the real world, people look out for VPN for accessing the restricted

contents which are banned in various countries and areas such as torrent. If you want a VPN for just surfing the restricted form of contents, you can download one from the internet according to your requirement.

How does a VPN work?

When you start by connecting any of your devices such as tablet, smartphone, laptop or desktop with the VPN, your device system will begin to behave as it is also from the same local form of network as the server of the VPN. The set of network traffic will be passed across a secure form of connection directly to the VPN. As your system will behave as if it is also from the similar network as the server, it will allow you to access all the resources of that same local

Kali Linux

network in a highly secure way when you are accessing it from some other part of the world. You can also surf the internet as if you were present at the exact location of the VPN which comes with some additional form of privileges if you are using any public Wi-Fi or if you want to access any type of website which is geo-restricted.

While you start browsing the internet by being connected with the Virtual Private Network, your device will contact the network of the VPN while absolutely secured and encrypted in nature. VPNs help by forwarding the requests of the users and then bring back the response of the website across the secure connection. For instance, in case you are using a VPN from the UK for accessing Netflix contents, Netflix will see that your connection is coming from any state of the UK only.

You can also access any business network while you are on the go. While you connect with any business network while travelling, the local network resources are not at all required to be exposed to the Web and it also helps by improving the security of your business network.

Chapter 10: Introduction to Wireless Networking

While talking about networking, one of the most trending topics is wireless networking. It has allowed people to reach new heights of reliability, along with benefits which allow them to use the internet with their devices without any form of cable or wire in between. All of these have been possible only because of wireless networking. In wireless networking, all the devices connect with a network switch or router which helps in establishing connection between the devices and the Web via radio waves. All the information and connection are established through the air.

Thus, it can be regarded as a mobile form of network where you are no longer required to be seated in one single place for surfing the internet. Wireless networking comes with some very interesting features which will be discussed further in this chapter. So, let's start with wireless networking and its various features.

Hacking and Penetration Testing with Kali Linux

Each and every organization and company comes with certain weak points which might turn out to be malicious. Such weak points can also lead to some

Kali Linux

serious form of attack which can be later used for manipulation of organizational data.

The only thing that you are left with which can ultimately help you in preventing all forms of hackers from getting into your systems is regular checking of infrastructure security. You will also need to ensure that no form of vulnerability is present within the infrastructure. For serving all of these functions, penetration testing is something which can ultimately help you. It helps in detecting the vulnerabilities within a system and forwards the same information to the organization administrators for filling up the gaps. Penetration testing is always performed within a highly secure and real environment which helps in finding out the real form of vulnerabilities and then helps to secure the system.

Details about penetration testing

It is a process which is used for testing of the systems for finding out whether any third party can penetrate the system or not. Ethical hacking is often mixed up with penetration testing as both of them somewhat serve the similar purpose and also functions more or less in the same way. In penetration testing, the pen tester scans the systems for any form of system vulnerability, flaws, risks and malicious content. You can perform penetration testing either in an online form of environment or server or even in a computer system. Penetration testing comes with the ultimate form of

Kali Linux

agendas: strengthening the system's security and defending the structure of an organization from potential attacks and threats.

Penetration testing is absolutely legal and is done along with the other official workings. When used in the proper and way, penetration testing has the ability of performing wonders. You can also consider penetration testing as a potential part of ethical hacking. You will need to perform the penetration tests at a regular intervals as it can improve the system capabilities. It also helps in improving cyber security. In order to find all the weak points within a program, system or application, various forms of malicious content are created by the pen testers. For an effective form of testing, the harmful form of content is spread across the overall network for the testing of vulnerability.

The technique used by penetration testing might not handle all the security concerns, but it can help to minimize the chances of attacks on the system. Penetration testing ensures that an organization or company is absolutely safe from all forms of threats and vulnerabilities and it helps in providing security from the cyber attacks. It also makes sure that the system of defense of an organization is working properly and is also enough for the company or organization to prevent the attacks and threats. It also indicates the security measures which are required to be changed by the organization to defend the system from attacks and vulnerabilities. All the reports regarding penetration testing are handed over to the system administrators.

Kali Linux

Metasploit

Metasploit is nothing but a framework meant for penetration testing which actually makes the concept of hacking much easier. It is regarded as an important tool for the majority of the attackers along with the security defenders. All you need to do is to just point Metasploit at the target, pick any exploit of your choice, choose the payload which you want to drop and just hit Enter. However, it is not that casual in nature and so you will need to start from the beginning. Back in the golden days, the concept of penetration testing came with lots of repetitive forms of labor which is now being automated by the use of Metasploit.

What are the things that you need? Gathering of information or gaining of access or maintaining the levels of persistence or evading all forms of detection? Metasploit can be regarded as the Swiss knife for hackers; if you want to opt for information security as your future career then you are required to know this framework in detail. The core of the Metasploit framework is free in nature and also comes pre-installed with the software Kali Linux.

How to use Metasploit?

Metasploit can seamlessly integrate itself with SNMP scanning, Nmap and enumeration of Windows patch along with others. It also comes with a bridge to the Tenable's scanner of vulnerability along with Nessus. Most of the

Kali Linux

reconnaissance tools which you can think of can integrate along with Metasploit and thus it makes it possible to find the

strongest possible point in the shield of security. After you have identified the weakness in a system, you can start hunting across the huge and extensible database for a point of exploit which will help in cracking the strongest armor and will let you in the system. Just like the combination of cheese and wine, you can also pair an exploit with the payload for suiting any task at hand.

Most of the hackers are looking out for a shell. It is a proper payload at the time of attacking a system based on Windows which acts as the Meterpreter and also as an in-memory form of interactive shell. Linux comes with its own set of shellcodes which depends on the exploit being used. Once within a target machine, the quiver of Metasploit comes with a complete suite of post-exploitation tools which also includes escalation of privileges, pass the hash, screen capture, packet sniffing, pivoting and keylogger tools. If you want you can also easily set up a proper form of backdoor if the target machine gets rebooted somehow.

Metasploit is loaded up with more and more features each year along with a fuzzer for identifying the potential flaws of security in the binaries as well as a too long list of the modules which are of auxiliary nature. What we have discussed till now is only a high-level vision of what can be done with Metasploit. The overall framework is modular in nature and can be extended

Kali Linux

easily and it also enjoys an active form of community. If it is not doing what you want, you can easily tweak it to meeting your needs.

How can you learn Metasploit?

You can find various cheap as well as free resources for the purpose of learning Metasploit. The best way of starting with Metasploit is by downloading Kali Linux followed by the installation along with a virtual machine for practicing on the target.

The organization which maintains Kali Linux and also runs the OSCP certification, Offensive Security, offers a free course that includes training of Metasploit and is known as Metasploit Unleashed.

Where can you download Metasploit?

Metasploit can be found along with the hacking software Kali Linux. But, if you want you can also download it separately from the official website of Metasploit. Metasploit can be used on the systems which are based on Windows and *nix. You can find out the source code of Metasploit Framework on GitHub. Metasploit is also available in various forms on the internet.

Kali Linux

Datastore

The datastore can be regarded as a core element of the Metasploit Framework. It is nothing but a table of several named values which allows the users to easily configure the component behavior within Metasploit. The datastore allows the interfaces to configure any of the settings, exploits for defining the parameters and also payloads for the purpose of patching the opcodes. It also allows Metasploit Framework to pass internally between the options of modules. You can find two types of datastores, the Global datastore which can be defined by using 'setg' and the Module datastore which can be defined at the modular level of datastore by using 'set'.

SQL Injection and Wi-Fi Hacking

When it comes to cyber attacks, one of the most widely used forms is the SQL Injection attack. In this, an attacker executes threat or invalid form of SQL statements which are used for database server control for an application of the web. It is also used for modifying, deleting or adding up records within the database without even the user knowing anything about it. This ultimately compromises the integrity of the data. The most important step which can be taken for avoiding or preventing SQL injection is by input validation.

Kali Linux

SQL Injection and its types

There are various types of SQL injection which you can find today. Let's have a look at them.

- **Classic or In-band SQL injection:** 1. Error based: Attackers employ the generated error by the database to attack the database server.

    2. Union based: In this UNION SQL operator is employed for combining a response for returning to the HTTP response.

- **Inferential or Blind SQL injection:** 1. Based on Boolean: It is based on return of true or false.

    2. Time based: It sends out SQL injection which forces the database just before responding.

- **Out of band SQL injection:** This takes place when an attacker is unable to use the similar form of channel for attacking and gathering the results.

Tools used for SQL injection

There are various tools which are used for carrying out SQL injection.

- SQLMap: This tool is used for an automatic form of SQL injection and it helps in taking over the database.

- jSQL Injection: It is a Java based tool which is used for SQL injection.
- Blind-SQL-BitShifting: It is used for blind SQL injection by the use of BitShifting.
- BBQSQL: It is a blind form of SQL injection exploitation tool.
- explo: It is a format of machine and human readable web vulnerability testing.
- Whitewidow: It is a scanning tool which is used for checking out the vulnerabilities of the SQL database.
- Leviathan: It acts as an audio toolkit.
- Blisqy: It is used for the purpose of exploiting time-based SQL injection within the headers of HTTP.

Detection tools for SQL injection

A tool named Spider testing tool is widely used for the purpose of identifying the holes of SQL injection manually by the use of POST or GET requests. If you can resolve the vulnerabilities within the code then you can easily prevent the SQL injections. You can also use a web vulnerability scanner for identifying all the defects within the code and for fixing the same to prevent SQL injection. The firewalls present in the web application or within the application layer can also be used extensively for preventing any form of intrusion.

Kali Linux

Hacking of Wi-Fi

Wi-Fi, or wireless networking, is the most preferred medium which is used for the purpose of network connectivity in today's world. However, because of its popularity, the wireless networks are also subjected to various attacks, along with several issues of security. If the attacker gains complete access to the network connection then the attacker can sniff off the data packets from any nearby location. The attackers employ sniffing tools for finding out the SSIDs and then hacks the Wi-Fi or wireless networks. After successful hacking, the attackers can monitor all the devices which are connected with the same SSID of the network. If you use authentication of WEP then it might be subject to dictionary attack. The attackers employ the RC4 encryption algorithm for the purpose of creating stream ciphers which are easily cracked. In case you are using authentication of WPA, then it might be subject to DOS along with dictionary attacks.

Tools for hacking of Wi-Fi

For the purpose of cracking WEP, the attackers use various tools such as WEPcrack, Aircrack, Kismet, WEPDecrypt and many others. For cracking WPA, tools such as Cain, Abel and CowPatty are used by the hackers. There are also other tools which are used in general for hacking of wireless network systems like wireshark, Airsnort, Wifiphisher, Netstumbler and many others. Even the attackers are now able to hack the mobile phone platform via the wireless network system. Android can be regarded as the most found mobile

Kali Linux

phone based platform but it is also very much susceptible to some specific types of vulnerabilities which ultimately makes it easier for the attackers to exploit the device security and then steal data from it. The most dangerous threats for the mobile devices are third party applications, email Trojans, wireless hacking and SMS.

How are Wi-Fi attacks carried out?

Most of the wireless network attacks are carried out by setting up rogue Access Points.

- **Evil Twin attack:** In this, the hacker sets up a false access point with the same name as that of the corporate AP which is close to the premises of the company. When any employee of the company connects to that access point, that employee unknowingly gives out all the details of authentication of the actual access point. Thus, the hacker can easily compromise the overall connection.
- **Signal jamming:** The hackers can easily disrupt the network connection which can be done by jamming the network signals. This is done by various tools which are used for creating noise.
- **Misconfiguration attack:** When the router of a network is set up by using a default form of configuration, weak form of encryption, weak credentials and algorithms, an attacker can easily crack the network.

- **Hotspot attack:** The attackers set up false hotspots or access points with the same name of the SSID similar to any public Wi-Fi access point. When any user connects with that access point unknowingly, the hackers can easily get access to the actual network.

How to Carry Out an Effective Attack

The term 'hacking' doesn't mean that it has to be negative all the time. You will have a proper idea about the overall process of hacking only when you will have a clear perception about the process behind it. Not only will you be able to learn about the process of hacking, but you will also be able to make your system much more protected from external attacks. Most of the time, when an attacker tries to gain access to a server of an organization or a company, it is generally done by using 5 proper steps. Let's have a look at those steps.

- **Reconnaissance:** This can be regarded as the very first step in the hacking process. During this phase, the attacker uses all the available means for the purpose of collecting all forms of relevant information about the primary target system. The relevant set of information might include the proper identification of the target, DNS records of the server, range of the IP address which is in target, the network and various other aspects. In simple terms, the attacker tries to collect all sorts of information along with the contacts of a website or server. This can be done by the attacker by the use of several forms of search engines like maltego or by researching about the system which is the target or by using the various tools like HTTPTrack to download a complete website for enumeration at a later stage.

By performing all these steps, the attacker will be able to determine the names of all the staffs within an organization very easily, find out the designated posts along with the email addresses of the employees.

- **Scanning:** After collecting all the relevant information about the target, the attacker will now start with the process of scanning. During this phase, the attacker employs various forms of tools like dialers, port scanners, vulnerability scanners, sweepers and network mappers for the purpose of scanning the target website or server data. During this step, the attackers try to seek out all the information which can actually help in the execution of a successful attack such as the IP address of the system, the user accounts and the computer names within that server. Right after the hackers are done with scanning of basic information, they start to test the target network to find out the possible avenues of attack. They might also employ several methods for network mapping just like Kali Linux.

The hackers also search for any automatic email system by which they can mail the staff of the target company about some false form of query like mailing the company HR about a job query.

- **Access gaining:** This is the most important of all the steps. In this phase, the attacker designs the blueprint of the target network along with the help of all relevant information which is collected in the first and second steps. As the hackers are done with enumeration of data followed by scanning of the system, they will now move to the step of gaining access to the system which will be based on the collected information.

- For instance, the attacker might decide to use a phishing attack. The attackers will always try to play safe and might employ a very simple attack for gaining overall access to the system. The attacker might also penetrate into the system from the IT department shell. The hackers use phishing email by employing the actual email address of the company. By using this phishing email ID, the attacker will send out emails to the techs that will also contain some form of specialized program

  along with a phishing website for gathering information about the login passwords and IDs. For this, the attackers can use various methods such as phone app, website mail or something else and then asking the employees to login with their credentials into a new website.

As the hackers use this method, they already have a special type of program running in the background which is also called as Social Engineering Toolkit which is used for sending out emails with the address of the server to the users.

- **Maintaining access to the server:** After the attackers have gained access to the target server, they will try every possible means for keeping their access to the server safe for future attacks and for the purpose of exploitation. As the attacker now has overall access to the server, he might also use the server as his very own base for launching several other forms of attacks. When an attacker gains access to an overall system and also owns the system, such a system is called as zombie system. The hacker might also try to hide himself within the server by creating a new administrator account with which he can easily mingle with the system without anyone knowing about it. For keeping safe access to the system, the hacker traces out all those accounts which are not being used for a long time and then elevates the privileges of all those accounts to himself.

As the hacker makes sure that no one has sensed his presence within the system, he starts to make copies of all the data on that server along with the contacts, messages, confidential files and many more for future use.

Kali Linux

- **Clearance of tracks:** Right before starting with the attack, the hackers chalk out their entire track regarding the identity so that it is not possible for anyone to track them. The attackers begin by altering the system MAC address and then run their entire system via a VPN so that no one can trace their actual identity.

Kali Linux

Conclusion

As you have completed learning the teachings of this entire eBook, you now have a very clear perception of the concepts of hacking along with the processes linked with it. You must have also gained a lot of knowledge about the properties, functioning and usage of Kali Linux. After completing this book, you will also be able to frame up all the necessary tools along with the components needed for setting up a secure and safe server of network meant either for your business or for your personal use. Always keep one thing in mind; you are the one who is responsible for everything that happens with your network or server.

With the help of Kali Linux, plus its relevant tools, you will be able to have a complete grip over the interface of your network security. This whole eBook is not only about the aspects of Kali Linux, it also discusses the basics of networking along with its security. With the help of Kali Linux, you will be able to perform periodic penetration testing which will ultimately determine the security of your system.

So, if you are thinking about improving the security of your network server, then start right away with the help of this eBook along with Kali Linux. Remember, you are the one who can actually make or break the security wall of your network.

Kali Linux

If you find this book helpful for your business in any way, kindly leave a review on Amazon.

Kali Linux

BOOK 2

Kali Linux

Introduction

Kali Linux is the world's generally well-known entrance testing stage, utilized by security experts in a wide scope of specializations. This includes infiltration testing, crime scene investigation, figuring out, and helplessness appraisal. It is the perfection of long stretches of refinement and the aftereffect of a persistent development of the stage, from WHoppiX to WHAX, to Back Track, and now to a total entrance testing structure utilizing numerous highlights of Debian GNU/Linux and the dynamic open source network around the world.

Kali Linux has not been created to be a basic assortment of devices, but instead an adaptable structure that expert infiltration analyzers, security aficionados, understudies, and novices can modify to accommodate their particular needs.

Why This Book?

Kali Linux isn't just an assortment of different data security apparatuses that are introduced on a standard Debian base and pre-arranged to get you going immediately. To capitalize on Kali, it is critical to have an intensive comprehension of its amazing Debian GNU/Linux underpinnings (which bolster every one of those extraordinary devices) and figuring out how you can place them to use for you.

In spite of the fact that Kali is unequivocally multi-reason, it is basically intended to help in entrance testing.

- pag. 123

Kali Linux

The goal of this book isn't to assist you with feeling comfortable when you use Kali Linux. In addition to helping improve your comprehension and streamlining your experience so when you are occupied with an infiltration test and time is of the essence, you won't have to stress over losing valuable minutes to put in new programming or empower another system administration. In this book, we will acquaint you first with Linux. After that, we will jump further as we acquaint you with the subtleties of Kali.

Linux so you know precisely what is happening in the engine.

This is important information to have, especially when you are attempting to work under tight time limitations. It isn't unusual to require this amount of information when you are getting set up, investigating an issue, battling to twist an apparatus to your will, parsing yield from a device, or utilizing Kali in a bigger scale condition.

Is This Book for You?

In the event that you are anxious to jump into the mentally rich and unbelievably interesting field of data security, and have legitimately chosen Kali Linux as an essential stage, this book will help you in that voyage. It is written to help first-time Linux clients, and Kali clients trying to develop their insight about the underpinnings of Kali. It is also for individuals who have utilized Kali for a considerable length of time yet who are hoping to formalize their learning, grow their utilization of Kali, and fill in holes in their insight.

Kali Linux

Also, this book can fill in as a guide, specialized reference, and study help for those seeking the Kali Linux Certified Professional confirmation.

Terms

There are various basic terms that regularly come into use while examining infiltration testing. Various callings, specialized claims to fame, and even individuals from a similar group have somewhat various understandings of the terms utilized in this field. Hence, the accompanying terms and related definitions will be utilized in this book.

Entrance Testing, Pentesting

Entrance testing is the approach, procedure, and methodology utilized by analyzers inside explicit and affirmed rules to attempt to bypass a data frameworks insurance including vanquishing the coordinated security highlights of that framework. This sort of testing is related with evaluating the specialized, regulatory, and operational settings and controls of a framework.

Regular infiltration tests just evaluate the security of the data framework as it is manufactured. The objective system framework executives and staff might possibly realize that an infiltration test is occurring.

Red Team, Red Teaming

Kali Linux

Red Teams reproduce a potential enemy in procedure and methods.

These groups are regularly bigger than an infiltration testing group and have a lot more extensive experience. Infiltration testing itself is frequently a sub-component of a Red Team Exercise, however, these activities test different elements of an association's security device. Red Teams frequently assault an association through specialized, social, and physical methods. They regularly utilize similar procedures utilized by Black Hat Hackers to test the association or data frameworks securities against these antagonistic on-screen characters. Notwithstanding Penetration Testing, the Red Team will perform Social Engineering assaults, including phishing and lance phishing and physical assaults including dumpster jumping and lock picking to pick up data and access. By and large, the objective associations staff won't realize a Red Team Exercise is being directed.

Moral Hacking

An Ethical Hacker is an expert infiltration analyzer that assaults frameworks in the interest of the framework proprietor or association owning the data framework. For the motivations behind this book, Ethical Hacking is synonymous with Penetration Testing.

White Hat

Kali Linux

White Hat is a slang term for an Ethical Hacker or a PC security professional that believes in philosophies that improve the security of data frameworks.

Dark Hat

Dark Hat is a term that distinguishes an individual that utilizes specialized methods to sidestep a frameworks security without consent to carry out unethical actions. Entrance Testers and Red Team individuals regularly utilize the strategies utilized by Black Hats to mimic these people while directing approved activities or tests. Dark Hats direct their exercises without authorization and illicitly.

Dark Hat alludes to a specialized master that straddles the line between White Hat and Black Hat. These people regularly endeavor to sidestep the security highlights of a data framework without authorization, not for benefit but instead to make the framework overseers aware of found shortcomings. Dark Hats regularly don't have authorization to test frameworks, yet are generally not after money related additions.

Powerlessness Assessment, Vulnerability Analysis

A powerlessness examination is utilized to assess the security settings of a data framework. These kinds of appraisals incorporate the assessment of security patches applied to and missing from the framework. The Vulnerability Assessment Team, or VAT, can be outside of the data framework or part of the data framework's supporting staff.

Security Controls Assessment

- pag. 127

Kali Linux

Security Controls Assessments assess the data framework's consistency with explicit legitimate or administrative necessities. Instances of these prerequisites incorporate, yet are not restricted to, the Federal Information Security Management Act (FISMA), the Payment Card Industry (PCI), and Health Insurance Portability and Accountability Act (HIPAA). Security Control Assessments are utilized as a feature of the Body of Evidence (BOE) utilized by associations to approve a data framework for activity in a generation situation. A few frameworks require infiltration tests as a major aspect of the security control evaluation.

Noxious User Testing, Malicious User Testing
In Malicious User Testing, the assessors accept the job of believed insider acting malignantly, a vindictive client, or a maluser. In these tests, the assessor is given the certifications of an approved general or managerial client, typically as a test account. The assessor will utilize these qualifications to endeavor to sidestep security limitations remembering seeing archives and settings for a way the record was not approved, changing settings that ought not be changed, and raising their very own consents past the level the record ought to have. Malicious client testing recreates the activities of a maverick insider.

Social Engineering
Social Engineering assaults are typically hurtful to the data framework or client. The Social Engineer utilizes individuals' natural need to help other people to bargain their way into the data framework. Normal Social Engineering strategies include attempting to get help work area examiners to reset client account

passwords or have end clients uncover their passwords empowering the Social Engineer to sign in to accounts they are not approved. Other Social Engineering strategies incorporate phishing and lance phishing.

Phishing

In Phishing (articulated like angling), the social architect endeavors to get the focused-on individual to uncover individual data like client names, account numbers, and passwords. This is frequently done by utilizing legitimate looking, but phony, messages from partnerships, banks, and client care staff. Different types of phishing attempt to get clients to tap on fake hyperlinks that will enable vindictive code to be introduced on the objective's PC without their knowledge. This malware will be utilized to extract information from the PC or utilize the PC to assault others. Phishing ordinarily isn't focused at explicit clients yet might be everybody on a mailing list or with a particular email address expansion, for instance each client with a "@foo.com" augmentation.

Lance Phishing

Lance Phishing is a type of phishing in which the objective clients are explicitly recognized. For instance, the aggressor may discover the email address of the Chief Executive Officer (CEO) of an organization or other officials and just phish these individuals.

Dumpster Diving

Kali Linux

In Dumpster Diving, the assessor channels through refuse disposed of by framework clients searching for data that will prompt further comprehension of the objective. This data could be framework setups or settings, arrange charts, programming variants and equipment parts, and even client names and passwords. The term alludes to entering an enormous refuse holder, or "plunging" little office trash cans whenever the open door can produce rewarding data, too.

Live CD, Live Disk, or LiveOS

A live CD or live circle alludes to an optical plate that contains a whole working framework. These plates are helpful to numerous assessors and can be adjusted to contain explicit programming segments, settings, and instruments. While live circles are regularly found on Linux disseminations, a few Microsoft Windows forms have been discharged throughout the years. In view of the data framework's settings, live circles could be the main bit of hardware that the assessor or analyzer should bring to the appraisal as the objective framework's PCs can be booted to the live circle. This turns one of the data framework's resources against the framework itself.

Kali Linux

Kali Linux

- pag. 132

Kali Linux

Chapter 1: Kali History

Kali Linux is the latest live circle security appropriation discharged by Offensive Security. This present rendition has more than 300 security and entrance testing devices included, sorted into supportive gatherings frequently utilized by entrance analyzers and others evaluating data frameworks. Not at all like prior disseminations discharged by Offensive Security, Kali Linux utilizes the Debian 7.0 conveyance as its base. Kali Linux proceeds with the genealogy of its antecedent, Backtrack, and is upheld by a similar group. As indicated by Offensive Security, the name change connotes the organization's complete revamp of the Backtrack dissemination. The tremendous enhancements over prior versions of the Backtrack appropriation justified an adjustment in name that shows this isn't only another rendition of Backtrack. Backtrack itself was an improvement over the two security devices it received from White Hat and SLAX (WHAX) also, Auditor. In this line, Kali Linux is the most recent manifestation of the business security examining and infiltration evaluation devices.

Downloading and Installing Kali Linux
Data IN THIS CHAPTER - This section will disclose how to get Kali Linux, one of the most dominant entrance testing tool boxes accessible.

Part OVERVIEW AND KEY LEARNING POINTS - This section will clarify the downloading and introducing process of Kali
Linux on:

- pag. 133

Kali Linux

Hard drives
Thumb drives (USB memory sticks)
SD cards

Kali Linux

Introducing working frameworks, for example, Microsoft's Windows, Apple's OS X, or open source stages like Debian and Ubuntu, might be natural to a few, however an update on this procedure is necessary. Those that have never introduced a working framework before ought not stress, the accompanying areas in this section will explain how to find, download, and introduce Kali Linux.

Kali Linux is remarkable from numerous points of view. However, the most significant qualifications of this conveyance are the capacity to run from a hard drive establishment as well as boot as a live plate and the number and kind of specific applications introduced as a matter of course. A live circle is a working framework introduced on a plate including Compact Disks (CDs), Digital Video Disk (DVD), or Blu-Ray Disk. As an entrance analyzer, the capacity to boot a live circle is very significant.

Those with access to neighborhood machines on the system can use live circles to utilize these machines regardless of whether the entrance analyzer doesn't have a record on the introduced working framework. The framework will boot to the live plate rather than the neighborhood hard drive; that is, on the off chance that the machine is arranged accurately the infiltration analyzer will, at that point, approach a large number of the assets on the nearby system, while simultaneously not leaving proof on the nearby machines hard drive. The product introduced on Kali Linux is extraordinarily equipped for the entrance analyzer. Of course, Kali Linux has 400 infiltration testing and security instruments, bundles and applications introduced and can include more as they are required.

Framework Information

Every working framework has slight deviations that will show up through their underlying establishment and arrangement; notwithstanding, most Linux/Unix-based stages are generally comparative in nature. When introducing Kali Linux, similarly as with other Linux working frameworks, arranging before establishment is pivotal. The following is a short rundown of interesting points when introducing Kali Linux.

- Will the working framework run on a PC or workstation?

- What size hard drive is required?

- Does the accessible hard drive have adequate space accessible?

- What number hard drive parcels are required?

- Is the executives log a worry?

- Is security a worry?

Choosing a Hardware Platform for Installation

Kali Linux

Customarily, the working framework is introduced on the PC's hard drive. With working frameworks, for example, Kali Linux, there is a capacity to introduce the working framework to thumb drives (otherwise known as glimmer drives) and SD cards because of the ongoing accessibility, and reasonableness of bigger limit gadgets. Despite the capacity utilized to introduce the working framework, it is important to decide to introduce it to an independent PC, (for example, a lab PC) or a PC that will consider a versatile arrangement.

In the event that certain equipment, like powerful illustrations cards, will be utilized for splitting passwords, it is suggested that the establishment of Kali Linux be introduced on a personal computer. On the off chance that there is a need to convey the working framework from client site to client site, or there is a longing to test remote gadgets, a PC is prescribed. The establishment of the working framework is the equivalent for PC and personal computers.

Hard Drive Selection

Not to over utilize the expression, however "Size does make a difference." A general guideline is: the bigger the drive, the better. This book is suggesting a drive with at least 120 GB of room. Even this can turn out to be full rapidly, particularly on account of secret phrase splitting and crime scene investigation or pentesting ventures that require a great deal of command over, proof, logs and report age or assortment. On account of general business and government security evaluations, the working framework is cleaned, deleted, or totally evacuated to keep up a set in

Kali Linux

benchmark condition. This training is broadly acknowledged all through the security network because of the requirement for a legitimate treatment of client classified information and limiting spillage of corporate data that might hurt the organization's reputation.

Apportioning the Hard Drive

Apportioning is the demonstration of isolating out the document framework to explicit parts of the hard drive by setting extraordinary square sizes and divisions. Parceling can keep a working framework from getting undermined by log documents that assume control over a framework and in specific situations give more prominent security. The working framework is, at the fundamental level, effectively broken into two distinct segments.

The primary segment is the swap territory, which is utilized for memory paging and capacity. A subsequent segment is assigned for everything else and is designed with a record structure, for example, the all-inclusive document framework 3 (ext3) or expanded document framework 4 (ext4). On PCs, particularly those gadgets where the working framework will be reloaded on numerous occasions, further dividing isn't important. For altered establishments or PCs that will have an increasingly steady working framework, there is a need to, in any event, separate out the brief (tmp) documents.

Propelled dividing of the hard drive and double booting a PC are outside the extent of this book and won't be secured. The main

Kali Linux

exemption is in Appendix A where redone circulations are presented with a thirdparty application called, Tribal Chicken.

Security During Installation

Kali Linux is an exceptionally versatile working framework with plenty of pre-introduced apparatuses that can pulverize PCs or arrange foundation. Whenever utilized inappropriately or dishonestly, it can also prompt activities that will be seen as criminal or law breaking. Consequently, passwords are basic. While passwords are the most fundamental security practice, numerous chairmen and security experts frequently overlook or disregard the utilization of passwords. Fundamental security practices, for example, legitimate utilization of passwords, are basic to guarantee that your establishment of Kali Linux isn't used by other people who may coincidentally or malevolently cause damage to an individual, PC, or system.

Downloading Kali

Kali Linux is a conveyance of Linux and is downloaded in an ISO (pronounced: eye-so) record. It should be downloaded from another PC and afterward consumed to a circle before establishment. At the time of writing this book, Kali Linux can be downloaded from http://www.kali.org/downloads/.

Documentation for cutting edge tasks, designs, and unique cases can likewise be found in Kali's legitimate site, http://www.kali.org/official-documentation/. There is likewise an exceptionally huge and dynamic network where clients can post

- pag. 138

Kali Linux

questions and help other people with challenges. Enlistment at this site is prescribed to access the network sheets that are overseen by Hostile Security, the creators of Kali Linux. Hostile Security will likewise convey messages about updates and network data.

Make certain to choose the correct design (i386 5 32-piece, amd64 5 64-piece). The trusted contributed pictures of Kali Linux are outside the scope of this book. If you wish to get acquainted with Kali, or need a sandbox domain for more noteworthy control, then the VMware download is ideal for those circumstances. Snap on the suitable download connection to proceed with your choice.

For Microsoft Windows 7 clients, double tap on the finished download and the Burn ISO Wizard will show up. Pursue the prompts to finish the transformation of ISO picture to a DVD that can be utilized for establishment. Linux clients should open the ISO in an appropriate plate consuming application, for example, K3b.

Kali Linux

Kali Linux

Chapter 2: Hard Drive Installation

The accompanying sections will give a literary and graphical establishment manage intended for straightforwardness. To effectively introduce Kali on the framework's hard drive, or even boot to the live circle, it is important that the Basic Input Output System (BIOS) be set to boot from optical plate. To start the establishment, place the CD in the PC's CD plate and boot the PC to the circle. Propelled clients alright with virtualization innovation, for example, VMware's Player or Oracle's Virtual box will likewise discover this guide direct and supportive to making a virtualized variant of Kali Linux.

Booting Kali with a PC booted to the Kali Linux circle effectively will show a screen that seems to be like a Figure. The rendition of Kali Linux being utilized for this guide is 1.0.5 64-Bit; variants downloaded at various occasions may look marginally changed; be that as it may, the graphical establishments are very comparable in nature. A refreshed guide for each new arrival of Kali Linux can be found at http://www.kali.org/ and it is strongly suggested to visit this site for the most recent documentation for your form before establishment or in case of questions.

Kali Linux is disseminated as a "Live CD" (otherwise known as Live ISO), which implies that the working framework can be run directly from the plate notwithstanding being introduced to a hard drive. Running Kali from the live circle enables the framework for sure and the entirety of the apparatuses will execute; be that as it may,

Kali Linux

the working framework displayed is non-determined. Non steady implies that once the PC is closed down, any memory, spared settings, archives, and potentially significant work or research might be lost. Running Kali in a non-determined state takes extraordinary consideration, propelled dealing with, and nice comprehension of the Linux directions and working framework. This technique is best for learning the Linux working framework without erasing the current working framework previously introduced on the PC's hard drive.

Another establishment that is out of the scope of this book, is Installation with Speech Synthesis. This is a fresher component to Kali and the Debian working framework. Establishment can be controlled vocally if you have equipment that supports discourse amalgamation. This book will concentrate on the graphical establishment for the present; in this manner, feature Graphical Install and press the Enter key.

Establishment—Setting the Defaults

The following screens will permit the choice of the framework's default language, area, and console language. Select the suitable settings and keep on propelling the installer. As the PC starts to pre-organize the establishment of Kali Linux, different advancement bars will come on the screen all through the establishment. Choosing the default settings is proper for the vast majority of those screens.

Establishment—Initial Network Setup

- pag. 142

Kali Linux

Figured subtleties the underlying arrangement and fundamental setup of the essential system interface card. Pick a host name by composing in the container and tapping on Continue. Host names ought to be one of a kind, as entanglements with systems administration can be a consequence of PCs that were designed with a similar host name while on a similar system.

After choosing a host name and hitting the Continue button, the following screen will request the PC's completely qualified space name, FQDN. This is essential for joining space conditions and a bit much for most lab situations. For this guide, the FQDN was left deliberately clear and can be skirted by choosing the Continue button.

Passwords

The following brief in the wizard will request a root-level secret phrase. The default secret word is: toor; in any case, another secret key must be chosen that contains every one of the following: capitalized, lowercase, number, and image. The secret word ought to have no detectability to the client and not be effectively speculated. A secret word of at least 10 characters is recommended. For instance, if the client once played secondary school soccer, a password like soccer22 would not be prescribed. Passwords can be produced using varieties of basic expressions to build review. Here are a few instances of solid passwords:

- St0n(3)b@tt73 "Stone Battle"

- P@p3r0kCur5# "Paper, Rock, Curse"

Kali Linux

- m!gh7yP@jjjama% h "Forceful Pajamas"

When composing your secret phrase, it will appear as a progression of bullets.

This is typical and conceals your secret phrase from being shown on the PC screen. After entering the equivalent solid secret word twice, click on Continue to progress further into the program.

Arranging the System Clock shows the brief for choosing a time period zone. Click on the suitable time zone and the Continue button.

Apportioning Disks

There are such a significant number of approaches to arrange segments for setting up a Linux working framework that a whole book could be written on the subject. This guide will concentrate on the most essential establishment, Guided Partitioning.

A few pictures show the default settings to that are at first featured. There will be nothing to choose until a specific Figure. Right now, the establishment might be accelerated by clicking Proceed until apportioning is finished. It is shrewd to survey each progression of the establishment wizard.

A few pictures show various choices for dividing hard drives during the establishment. LVM, or Logical Volume Management, isn't suggested for workstation, thumb drive, or SD card establishment.

Kali Linux

LVM is for various hard drives, and is prescribed distinctly for cutting edge clients. "Guided—client whole circle," ought to be chosen. Click on Continue to progress through the establishment procedure. A figure shows the hard drive that has been chosen for establishment.

Contingent upon your equipment and form of Kali Linux, the establishment experience may contrast somewhat. The hard drive will be chosen for; if needed, click on the Continue button to progress through the establishment procedure. As this book is designed for new clients of the Kali Linux dispersion: "All records in a single parcel (suggested for new clients)" is the best alternative and ought to be chosen. Click on the Continue button to progress through the establishment procedure.

At this point in the wizard, the parcel direct has been finished and is introduced for your survey. An essential parcel containing the entirety of the framework, client, and scripting documents will be made as one segment. A subsequent segment is made for swap space. The swap zone is virtual framework memory that pages records
to and from the PC's focal preparing unit (CPU) and arbitrary access memory (RAM). All Linux frameworks are prescribed to have a swap zone and the general practice is to set the swap zone equivalent to or one and a half times the measure of physical RAM introduced on the PC. As found in the figure, "Get done with parceling and compose changes to circle," will be chosen for you. Click on Continue to progress through the establishment

- pag. 145

procedure. Some figure is a last possibility audit for parceling before the hard drive arrangement is submitted. There are approaches to change segment estimates later on if needed, yet doing so might cause enormous harm to your working framework if not done accurately. This brief in the wizard is an admonition that you are going to compose information to a predefined hard drive with

the recently characterized parcel tables. Select YES and click on Continue to progress through the establishment procedure.

After clicking Continue at the last brief of the parceling area of the wizard, the hard drive segment will start. An A figure shows that the genuine establishment is being led as of now. Depending upon the equipment you have, this procedure can take only a few moments to an hour or more.

Arrange the Package Manager

The bundle supervisor is an essential piece of the working framework's arrangement. The bundle supervisor alludes to the update vault where Kali Linux will pull updates and security patches. It is prescribed to utilize the system reflect that accompanies the Kali Linux ISO as this will the most state-of-the-art hotspots for bundle the executives. The figure shows that "YES" will be chosen. Click on the Continue button to progress through the establishment procedure.

In the case of utilizing an intermediary, enter the arrangement data where fitting on the following brief in the wizard or leave it blank. Click on Continue.

Kali Linux

Introducing the GRUB Loader

The Grand Unified Bootloader (GRUB) is the primary screen that will be shown each time the PC is begun. This permits the check of specific settings at boot, make on the fly changes, and make setting modifications before the working framework loads. While GRUB isn't fundamental for some propelled clients, it is strongly suggested for most establishment types. Click on "YES" to introduce the GRUB, then click on Continue.

Finishing the Installation

Presently remove the plate from the PC and reboot. When prompted, do as such and afterward click on the Continue catch to complete the establishment.

After rebooting, the Welcome screen will be exhibited. Sign in as the root client with the predefined password set earlier in the establishment procedure. Welcome to Kali Linux!

Thumb Drive Installation

USB memory gadgets, regularly alluded to as thumb drives, are simply a capacity gadget that is joined through a USB interface to the PC. This book suggests utilizing a USB gadget with at least 8GB of space, ideally considerably more. New PCs can boot to USB gadgets. If this alternative is chosen, ensure that the PC being utilized can bolster booting from a USB gadget.

The accompanying areas separate the establishment of Kali Linux on to USB utilizing a Microsoft Windows PC or Linux stage. Make

Kali Linux

certain to check the documentation given on the Official Kali Linux landing page for updates to this procedure.

With regards to thumb drives being utilized as bootable gadgets, there are two key terms that are significant: determination and non-persistence. Constancy alludes to the capacity of your gadget to hold any composed or adjusted records after the machine is turned off. Non- persistence alludes to the gadget losing all settings, customizations, and records if the machine reboots or is turned off. Explicitly for this book, the thumb drive establishment of Kali Linux from a Windows stage will be non-persistent, and the establishment from a Linux stage will be constant.

Windows (Nonpersistent)

Required application—Win32 Disk Imager: http://sourceforge.net/ventures/win32diskimager/

Before downloading the Kali Linux ISO, put a thumb drive in the PC and wait for it to be identified by Windows, observing the drive letter relegated. Next open Win32 Disk Imager. Click on the envelope symbol to peruse and choose the Kali ISO document and afterward click the "alright" button. Select the right drive letter from the gadget drop-down menu. At long last click the "State" button.

When Win32 Disk Imager has finished consuming the ISO, reboot the PC and select the thumb drive from the BIOS POST menu. Most

Kali Linux

makers have various strategies for booting to USB gadgets; make certain to check the PC producer's documentation.

Linux (Persistent)

When constructing a steady thumb drive, again, size does make a difference! The greater the thumb drive capacity, the better. Additionally, contingent upon the rendition of Linux in which you will assemble this USB gadget, be certain that the application GParted is introduced. Check your working framework's documentation if you are experiencing issues introducing GParted. One of the accompanying techniques might be fundamental for your Linux establishment if GParted isn't introduced:

- well-suited get introduce gparted

- fitness introduces gparted

- yum introduce gparted

Subsequent to downloading the Kali Linux ISO, plug in your thumb drive. Open a terminal window and confirm the USB gadgets area the accompanying direction. mount j grep - I udisks jawk '{print $1}'

Shows that the yield of the order as "/dev/sdb1." The USB gadget's yield might be diverse dependent on the PCs settings and design. In the following order, swap "sdb" to coordinate the right distinguishing proof and evacuate any numbers toward the end. Utilize the "dd" order to move the Kali ISO picture to the USB

Kali Linux

gadget. dd if 5 kali_linux_image.iso of 5/dev/sdb bs 5 512k Now dispatch Gparted. gparted/dev/sdb. The drive should as of now have one parcel with the picture of Kali that was simply introduced.

Add another parcel to the USB by choosing New, from the menu that shows up in the wake of clicking on the Partition menu from the File Menu Bar. Slight deviations in yield can be available from various gadget producers. By and large, the means are like the following:

- Click on the dim "unallocated" space.

- Click on "New" from the Partition drop-down menu.

- Use the sliders or physically determine drive size.

- Set the File System to ext4.

- Click Add.

- From the primary window select, Apply All Operations from the Edit dropdown menu.

- Click Okay when prompted. This may take some time.

To include constant usefulness utilize the accompanying order. mkdir/mnt/usb mount/dev/sdb2/mnt/usb reverberation "/association".. /mnt/usb/persistence.confumount/mnt/usb

- pag. 150

Kali Linux

Formation of the LiveUSB is currently finished. Reboot the PC and boot from the thumb drive.

SD Card Installation

Micro computing gadgets, for example, the RaspberryPi and Google's Chrome Notebook, are fit for running on SD cards. These little gadgets can be utilized for plenty of purposes; a person is just restricted by their very own creative mind. The best of the gadgets, for example, the Raspberry Pi, is that they are modest and an enormous hit in the open source networks making assets promptly accessible to tinkerers all over the place.

There is one disadvantage to the introducing Kali Linux on ARM gadgets; the pictures are custom and must be characterized for each bit of equipment.

Pictures for ARM gadgets can be situated on Kali's legitimate download pages, http://www.kali.org/downloads/. Check whether your equipment has an upheld picture accessible for download.

The following gives a short manual for introducing Kali Linux to good ARM engineering-based gadgets.

1. Download the suitable picture from Kali's legitimate site (http://www.kali.org/downloads/).

2. Add a blank SD card. Confirm the mounted area with the accompanying direction. mount j grep - I vfat (Assuming/dev/sdb for the following stage.)

Kali Linux

3. Move the Kali.img document to the SD card. dd if 5 kali.img of 5/dev/sdb bs 5 512k

4. Unmount and match up any compose tasks before extracting the gadget. umount/dev/sdb adjust

5. Extract the SD card.

6. Supplement the SD card containing the Kali Linux picture into your ARM engineering registering gadget and boot to the SD card.

In this section, the themes secured will enable the client to introduce Kali Linux to most PCs, workstations, thumb drives, and smaller scale figuring gadgets. Introducing Kali Linux is a lot of like riding a bike; do it once, and you won't generally ever forget how to introduce Kali in the future. Check with the documentation and network message sheets on Kali's authentic site for new updates, variants, and advancements created in the security network. Connecting up and coordinating with other security experts, specialists, and programmers can, and will, grow the psyche, help you dive further into new tasks, and aid answer addresses when capable.

Programming, Patches, and Upgrades

Data IN THIS CHAPTER

- APT Package Handling Utility

Kali Linux

- Debian Package Manager

- Tar-balls

- A Practical Guide to Installing Nessus

Section OVERVIEW AND KEY LEARNING POINTS - This part will explore the procedure important for looking after, updating, and introducing custom and outsider applications utilizing APT bundle dealing with utility (adept get) and the Debian bundle supervisor (dpkg).

Kali Linux

- pag. 154

Kali Linux

Chapter 3: Well-Suited Package Handling Utility

The APT bundle dealing with utility, known as "able get," is a lightweight and amazingly incredible order line device for introducing and evacuating programming bundles. Able get monitors everything introduced alongside the required conditions, which are the extra programming bundles required for appropriate usefulness of other programming. For example, Metasploit, the pentester's closest companion, depends on a specific programming language called Ruby. Without Ruby introduced, Metasploit couldn't dispatch; subsequently, Ruby is a reliance of Metasploit.

Able get does not just monitor the conditions for introduced programming. It will monitor forming and entomb conditions when updates are accessible. At the point when programming bundles are never again valuable or deteriorated well-suited get will caution the client at the next refresh and prompt to expel old bundles.

Able get can be an extremely basic or exceptionally involved apparatus. The organization of bundles is pivotal to ensuring Kali Linux works appropriately and that product bundles are state-of-the-art. While the average client of Kali Linux doesn't have to know the inside operations of well-suited get, there are a few rudiments that each client should know.

Introducing Applications or Packages

Introducing extra programming is the most essential capacity of the able get order and is straightforward. The linguistic structure

Kali Linux

below will give an example of the fundamental use of the introduce subcommand:

adept get introduce {package_name}

Take a stab at introducing "gimp;" a picture altering programming bundle: well-suited get introduce gimp

Update

Now and again the sources, or vaults, should be checked for updates to different applications and bundles introduced on Kali Linux. Updates should be checked before introducing any new bundles, and is needed before playing out a move up to the working framework or programming applications or bundles. The punctuation for performing refreshes pursues: adept get update

Redesign

No framework is ever great. Each major working framework is in a consistent condition of progress, improvement, and fixing the executives to offer new highlights or fix bugs. The update capacity will pull down and introduce all new bundled variants of new introduced programming bundles. The magnificence of all Linux based working frameworks is that they're open source, implying that anybody on the planet can submit new code to the dispersion directors of the working framework to help improve the usefulness of the framework for bug detection or a requirement for development. This takes into account patches to be refreshed quicker contrasted with the corporate monsters like Microsoft. As expressed before, it is necessary to install an update before

Kali Linux

running an overhaul. To update Kali utilize the accompanying direction:

adept get update

Appropriation Upgrade

The appropriation update work works comparably to the overhaul work. This capacity likewise searches out hotspots for extraordinary stamped bundles and their conditions just as new bundles the dissemination directors have assigned to be incorporated with the most current gauge. For instance, while conjuring the circulation overhaul work, the whole form of Kali will be raised from variant 1.0 to rendition 1.n, or 2.n, etc. Use the accompanying language to update Kali: well-suited get dist-update

Expel

Able get can be utilized to diminish the impression of a framework, or when evacuating free of a particular program. It is additionally recommended that all bundles not being used, those not filling a need, or redundant for your working framework, be uninstalled. For instance, if the Leaf cushion application isn't required on the framework, at that point expel it. If the application should be introduced later, it tends to be, notwithstanding, it is ideal to forget about what is pointless. The accompanying language can be utilized to expel an application or bundle: able get expel {package_name}

Have a go at expelling "leafpad" and afterward reinstalling the application:

- pag. 157

Kali Linux

able get expel leafpad

able get introduce leafpad

Auto Remove

After some time, the working framework's application bundles are supplanted with better than ever forms. The auto expel capacity will expel old bundles that are never again required for the best possible usefulness of the framework. It is prescribed that the auto expel work be pursued before an overhaul or appropriation update. Utilize the accompanying language to run auto evacuate:

able get autoremove

Cleanse

What is the distinction between expel and cleanse? The expel capacity won't demolish any design documents, and leaves those things on your hard drive in the event that the records are required later. This is valuable, particularly with applications, for example, MySQL, Samba Server, or Apache. The setup records are critical for the operability of your applications. Sometimes, it is important to expel the entirety of the application documents, even design records for that application, from the framework so as to re-introduce applications to a clear state and begin once again, or clear all hints of potentially delicate data. Cleansing an application from the framework will totally eradicate the application bundle and all related setup records in a single motion.

Kali Linux

Be careful to not get too careless when utilizing the cleanse work; it is hazardous when utilized inaccurately or on an inappropriate application as all related records will be expelled from the framework. Cleanse can be utilized with the accompanying language structure: well-suited get cleanse {package_name}

Clean

Bundles are downloaded to the framework from their source, unpackaged, and afterward introduced. The bundles will live on the framework until further notice.

These bundles are never again fundamental after establishment of the application. After some time, these bundles can gobble up plate space and should be cleaned away. The accompanying linguistic structure can be utilized to start the perfect capacity: able get spotless

Autoclean

Autocleaning additionally cleans the framework along these lines as the perfect capacity. It ought to be used for overhaul and conveyance moves up to the framework, as the autoclean capacity will evacuate old bundles that have been supplanted with new ones. For example, assume application Y form 1 was introduced on the framework and after a move up to the framework, application Y v1 is supplanted with application Y v2. The autoclean capacity will just clean away form 1, while, the perfect capacity will expel the application bundles for the two variants. The following language structure will begin the autoclean work: adept get autoclean

- pag. 159

Kali Linux

Assembling It All

Organization of bundles is tied in with working more efficiently. The following are the accompanying directions that a client can use to ensure that the entirety of the potential fixes, bundles, and updates are forward-thinking and all set:

1. well-suited get update && adept get redesign && well-suited get dist-overhaul

2. well-suited get autoremove && adept get autoclean

The "&&" passage on the order line considers numerous directions to run successively.

Debian Package Manager

The significant flavors (or disseminations) of Linux have singular application bundling frameworks. Kali Linux was based over the Debian 7.0 base working framework, and may require outsider applications, like Tenable's Nessus.

Nessus is a weakness-examining application that can be introduced from prepackaged documents appropriate for the Debian Package Manager. The utilization of Nessus will be explored in the section on examining. While downloading these sorts of uses, search for the ".deb" document expansion toward the finish of the record name.

Kali Linux

There is no advantage of utilizing the Debian Package Manager over APT. The aptget program was composed explicitly for the administration of Debian bundles.

Outside applications that must be purchased from a seller are not accessible freely and well-suited gets sources will be not able find the bundles for download and establishment. Kali Linux isn't equipped for handling RPM (Red Hat Packages) without additional product introduced, and the act of utilizing RPMs on a Debian-based framework isn't suggested.

Introduce

In the wake of downloading a .deb bundle, the dpkg direction should be utilized so as to introduce the bundle. Most .deb bundles are clear and contain the entirety of the conditions needed for the application to work effectively. In some cases, for the most part managing authorized programming, merchants may require extra strides before establishment and will by and large have guidelines for appropriate establishment on the framework. Make certain to check the seller's documentation before beginning the establishment:

dpkg - I {package_name.deb}/{target_directory}

Expel

Expelling a bundle (- r) or cleansing a bundle (- P) works in the generally same way that APT does and pursues a similar example for dealing with bundles: dpkg - r {package_name.deb}

Kali Linux

Cleansing a bundle with the Debian bundle chief works similarly to the evacuate work and can be started with the accompanying direction:

dpkg - p {package_name.deb}

Checking for Installed Package

One super power that APT doesn't have over the Debian Package Manager is the capacity to decipher the present status of introduced or evacuated programming. When utilizing the rundown work inside dpkg, the yield will show a few characters code toward the start of the line demonstrating the bundle's present condition of establishment. When run against the Leaf cushion application bundle, the accompanying picture shows that the bundle is evacuated, yet the arrangement documents are as yet accessible.

After the order dpkg - P leafpad is run, the bundle's design documents are likewise expelled. Figure 3.2 shows the comparing yield of the Leafpad application bundle when it has been totally cleansed from the framework. To search for the status of introduced or expelled programming, utilize this language structure: dpkg - l {package_name}

Progressively point by point data about the bundle introduced can be shown on the screen with the following order:

Give close consideration to the utilization of upper and lowercase. Lowercase "p" prints the data to the screen. The capitalized "P" will cleanse the bundle from the framework without asking, "Are you certain?"

Kali Linux

- pag. 163

Kali Linux

- pag. 164

Kali Linux

Chapter 4: Tarballas

Tar, starting in the yester long periods of Unix frameworks, was named for its capacity, which was at first for composing numerous documents to Tape Archives (TAR).

Not every person needs the capacity to move various records to tape. However, they might need the characteristic usefulness of the tar application which is to produce a holder document that will house different documents. This allows simpler shipping of documents. Moreover, these documents can be compacted with gunzip (gzip) diminishing their general size. A few bundles from outsider or opensource activities can be downloaded in tarball design and are effectively distinguished by the .tar record augmentation or .tar.gz for compacted tarballs.

During an infiltration test, a gigantic measure of filtering archives, screen catches, redid contents, and customer documentation are caught. Utilizing the Tarball framework takes into consideration simpler assortment, the board, and payment, everything being equal. It is additionally exceptionally recommended that all records from entrance tests be kept in a protected area for 5 years, or the date dictated by the legal time limit of the state where the work was performed. Clients may likewise have stipulations on maintenance prerequisites that ought to be explained in the infiltration tests rules of commitment (ROE). The ROE will be explored in the section on announcing. If an organization or contractual worker is exceptionally dynamic with infiltration testing,

Kali Linux

the measure of documentation can heap up rapidly and before long be wild. Tarball, particularly when compacted, gives an arrangement of control that keeps records separated and takes into consideration simpler reinforcement and administration.

Formation of a Tarball

Making a tarball record can be clear or complex. Keep in mind, the first capacity of the tar direction was intended to send records to TAR. For cutting edge use of the tarball framework, look at the manual pages for tarball (man tarball). For this book just the fundamental formation of tarball records will be incorporated; be that as it may, this data is helpful and can progress to pretty much any Linux-based stage. The following gives a look through the steps needed that a client can pursue to make an example tarball.

Make an index for your documents. For this situation the tar-demo1 catalog is being made with the mkdir order: mkdir tar-demo1

Next make various records in this index that can be utilized to delineate the tar direction. For this situation the correct carrot (.) will be utilized to make a record with the substance "Hi world." This document will be named record 1, and a number of records can be made in a similar way by changing the last number. Making the records along these lines will likewise move your documents into the registry indicated, for this situation tar-demo1: reverberation "Hi World". tar-demo1/file1 reverberation "Hi World". tar-demo1/record 2

Kali Linux

Change into the registry that you wish to make a tarball in. For this example it is the tar-demo1 index:

album tar-demo1

Produce another tarball with the documents contained inside the present catalog.

In this model the reference bullet (*) is utilized to mean everything in this registry ought to be added to the tar document:

tar - cf tarball-demo.tar *

The tar - tf order is utilized to list the substance of the tarball:
 tar - tf tarball-demo.tar

Extricating Files from a Tarball

The steps to removing records from a tarball are as simple as one, two, and three; be that as it may, the area of the data is put that is the key. The documents extricated from a tarball are set in the working registry. If a tarball is removed from the root index, that is the place the documents are going to wind up. It is prescribed that great propensities structure at the earliest opportunity; in this manner, all clients of tarballs should utilize the "- C" switch when extricating records. The "- C" switch enables the client to determine the area of where the documents need to go.

Make an index for the records to be extricated into. For this situation the registry made is named tar-demo2:

Kali Linux

mkdir/root/tar-demo2

Concentrate the records into the particular catalog:
tar - xf/root/tar-demo1/tarball-demo.tar - C/root/tar-demo2/

Ensure that all of the records are removed to the registry that was indicated in the prior advance:

ls/root/tarball-demo2/

Packing a Tarball

Tarballs can be packed during creation with numerous various sorts of calculations. One standard being used is gunzip, otherwise called gzip. This is finished with the accompanying directions.

Make a catalog for your documents. For this situation the tar-demo3 registry is made:
mkdir tar-demo3

Presently move your records into the index. As above the reverberation direction will be utilized to make the documents for this showing:
reverberation "Hi World". tar-demo3/file1

Change into the catalog that you wish to place your tarball. Again, in this model the tar-demo3 catalog is being utilized:
compact disc tar-demo3

Kali Linux

Create another tarball with the documents contained inside the present index.

This is finished using the - czf switches with the tar order. The switches on the tar direction guarantee the tarball is made accurately. The c switch makes another chronicle and the z guarantees the records are packed (or compressed) and the f switch means the name following the switches (tarball-demo.tar.gz) will be utilized as the name for the new document. Again, the reference mark (*) tells tar that everything in this index ought to be remembered for the new tar record:

tar - czf tarball-demo.tar.gz *

Posting the substance of the tarball is finished with the t and f switches. The t switch shows the record substance ought to be shown (or composed to the screen) and again the f switch demonstrates the document name will pursue the switches:

tar - tf tarball-demo.tar

Extraction of documents from a packed tarball works the very same route as extraction from a non-compacted tarball. The main change is the x switch is utilized to show that tar should remove the substance of the tarball. While it isn't required, it is standard practice to name the record with the .gz augmentation to show to others that the tarball is packed. Notice that the record in this model has two periods (.tar.gz); this is absolutely adequate in

Kali Linux

Linux situations and is standard with packed tar documents: tar - xf {tarball_file.tar.gz} - C {directory_for_files}

Kali Linux

Chapter 5: A Practical Guide to Installing Nessus

Viable, a well regarded name in the security network, has delivered a stunning application for defenselessness filtering called Nessus. There are two versions of the application that offer contrasting degrees of usefulness and backing. These are the Nessus Professional and Home forms. The Professional form offers significantly more modules for compliancy checking, SCADA, and arrangement checking and is amazing for group use. For this book, the establishment of the Nessus Vulnerability Scanner with the home feed will be utilized. Nessus is examined further in the part on filtering yet introducing Nessus now will concrete the information from this section.

Refresh and Clean the System Prior to Installing Nessus.
In a windows terminal type the following directions: well-suited get update && well-suited get redesign && able get dist-overhaul able get autoremove && well-suited get autoclean

Introduce and Configure Nessus

Download Nessus 5.0 or higher from http://www.nessus.org/download.

Select the Debian bundle for either 32-or 64-piece working framework. Peruse the membership understanding and click the Agree button. Nessus will not work if the understanding isn't

Kali Linux

acknowledged. Note the area where the document is being downloaded to as it will be needed to finish the establishment.

From a terminal window enter the accompanying:

dpkg - I B/{Download_Location}/Nessus-{version}.deb

A progressively far reaching arrangement guide can be found in Appendix some time setting up a pentesting domain structure with Tribal Chicken.

End

This section secured the basic abilities important for bundle the executives on the Kali Linux framework. Able is a ground-breaking order line apparatus that robotizes the administration of bundles, update, and fixes. The Debian Package Manager (dpkg) is the fundamental framework that APT was based over for bundling the executives. With the fundamental understanding and general acclimation of these instruments, anybody can stay up with the latest applications.

For cutting edge utilization of the instruments in this section, consult the manual pages either from inside a terminal window or online through their individual authority sites. These instruments can produce a domain ideal for any individual or pulverize a whole framework without a solitary brief or thought of regret. It is a very good idea that until a client is OK with the utilization of these

Kali Linux

apparatuses, that hands-on training ought to be practiced in a different framework or a virtual domain.

Designing Kali Linux

Data IN THIS CHAPTER - Using the default Kali Linux settings can be helpful for adapting yet it is frequently important to adjust essential settings to boost the utilization of this stage

Part Overview and Key Learning Points

This part will clarify

- the nuts and bolts of systems administration

- utilizing the graphical UI to arrange organize interfaces

- utilizing the direction line to design arrange interfaces

- utilizing the graphical UI to design remote cards

- utilizing the order line to design remote cards

- beginning, halting, and restarting the Apache server

- introducing an FTP server

- beginning, halting, and restarting the SSH server

- pag. 173

Kali Linux

- mounting outside media

- refreshing Kali

- redesigning Kali

- including the Debian store

ABOUT THIS CHAPTER - Networking is the way that PCs and other current electronic gadgets speak with one another. This can be viewed as streets between gadgets with rules and necessities (conventions), transit regulations (rule sets and arrangements), support groups (organize administrations), law enforcement (organize security), private streets (firewall ports and convention limitations—likewise part of security). In the following areas, the rudiments of systems administration will be portrayed as will the means that should be taken to appropriately design organizing in Kali.

Systems administration is a perplexing point, and this part scarcely starts to expose organizing. The clarification introduced here just serves to outline and disclose the segments required to effectively arrange the system parts of Kali Linux. To get an increasingly nitty gritty comprehension of systems administration look at *Networking Explained*, second ed., by Michael Gallo and William Hancock. This clarification will furnish the user with the fundamental comprehension of the most essential system segments.

Kali Linux

The Basics of Networking

Systems administration can be thought of as a progression of electronic streets between PCs. These streets can be physical, most normally copper class 5 or 6 (CAT 5 or CAT 6) links or fiber optic links. Remote systems administration utilizes unique radio transmitters and collectors to direct indistinguishable fundamental errands from physical systems.

Notwithstanding the medium, physical or remote systems administration has similar fundamental parts. First there are at least two gadgets that will communicate, for instance, Adam's PC will speak with Bill's PC. To do this, they will require the right interchanges gear working on the right medium. For this model, Adam will interface the equivalent physical CAT5-based system that Bill is associated with. If the settings are right, Bill could be utilizing a remote system card and Adam could be utilizing a wired system card as long as the conventions and settings for both are right. For this to work accurately both Adam and Bill should interface a similar system portion utilizing a gadget like a remote switch that would associate the diverse physical media types, wired and remote.

There are various parts that make up a cutting edge organize and completely clarifying systems administration is a long way past the scope of this book. The little system portion that will be disclosed will be adequate to depict how to arrange a system card. This little system is just two PCs that are being utilized by Adam and Bill, a wired switch associated with a link modem and the links that interface everything together (all CAT5 in this model). The switch has an inside Internet convention (IP) address of 192.168.1.1, which is very normal for little home office (SOHO) and home systems default setup. This little switch interfaces with the Internet through its outside association, utilizing an IP address allocated by the Internet Service Provider that will empower Adam and Bill to surf the web once they effectively arrange their system cards. In this model, the switch likewise gives dynamic host design convention (DHCP), essential firewall capacities, and space name administration (DNS), every one of these will be talked about in more detail later. This system is shown in Figure 4.3 and will be the base system utilized in the entirety of the accompanying parts.

Private Addressing

The interior interface (or system card) for the switch has an IP address of 192.168.1.1; this is what is known as a private location as it can't be utilized on the Internet. It is fine for the interior system spoke to by the dark box in a Figure similar to the addresses given by DHCP, like the IP address given to Adam and Bill's PCs. A table records the normal private IP that can be utilized for interior or private systems, however can't be utilized on the Internet.

To get to the Internet, the switch does a touch of enchantment called arrange address interpretation (NAT) that changes over the IP used by Adam and Bill to addresses that can be used on the Internet. This is ordinarily the location that is given to the switch by the digital Internet supplier and will be relegated to the outer interface (another system card). If a client was to attempt to utilize

Kali Linux

these addresses on the Internet, without a NAT switch, the correspondence would bomb as Internet switches and different gadgets dismiss these private IP addresses.

Default Gateway

The switch isolates these two systems, inside and outer, and gives some fundamental security capacities, similar to a simple firewall. Moreover, the switch gives an exit from the private system to general society arrange, regularly the Internet. Thus, the switch's interior interface IP address is the exit from Adam and Bill's system. This location, called the default passage, will be utilized later when designing the system cards for the client's two PCs. A decent method to picture the default door is to see it as the single street out of a community. Anybody needing to leave the town would need to know where this street is. On a system PCs (through the system card) need to know where the exit from the neighborhood organize is; this is the default entryway.

Name Server

PCs converse with one another in numbers, while individuals are vastly improved at speaking with words and expressions. For correspondence to work effectively, PCs regularly utilize name server or area name administration (DNS). This book will cover DNS in more prominent detail later, so just an outline of DNS will be talked about in this section. Fundamentally, the name server interprets human cordial names (like www.syngress.com) to an IP address that PCs and systems administration segments are better at working with. The DNS, synonymous with name server, gives

Kali Linux

interpretation between human benevolent and PC well-disposed locations. For instance, when a PC needs to speak with another PC, a web server for instance, it should initially interpret the intelligible location to a PC neighborly address that can be utilized to send the message. The individual would type www.syngress.com in their preferred program, and the PC would advance this location for goals to a DNS machine. The DNS would answer with the machine facilitating the website page's IP address (69.163.177.2). The client's PC would then utilize this IP address to speak with the Syngress web server and the client could cooperate with the Syngress website page. Without this administration, people would be required to remember each site's special IP Address. This would mean individuals would need to recall 69.163.177.2, not syngress.com. Manual design of a system card requires the distinguishing proof of a DNS or name server.

DHCP

For unadulterated system enchantment, nothing beats DHCP. With a PC set up for programmed setup of DHCP, the client should simply interface with a working system link and get down to business. This is done when the PC starts correspondence over the system, by conveying a communicate demand searching for a DHCP server. The server reacts to the customer and allocates organizing designs to the mentioning PC. This incorporates an IP address for the PC (just the system card, yet that is a little in the weeds for this clarification), the default entryway, name server—or name servers, and the default subnet cover.

Kali Linux

As a rule, this is an incredible method to arrange your system card. If you are leading an entrance test, utilizing DHCP to design your system card reports to everybody that you are entering the system, ordinarily not something to be thankful for.

Essential Subnetting

Subnetting is a subject that can confound many individuals, so for this book subnetting might be disclosed as the best approach to design organizes in the most ideal manner to spare IP addresses. This is finished by applying a cover that will sift through a portion of the PC's IP address permitting the systems tending to be revealed. Back to the Syngress model, the IP address is 69.163.177.2 and if we were on a little system that had under 255 clients we could utilize a class C subnet cover of 255.255.255.0. While applying the cover, portions of the location are counteracted and others remain, enabling the PCs on the system to know the system they are on. Again, a fundamental case of a subnet veil utilizes just the numbers 255 and 0 numbering octets; consequently, to distinguish the system, any piece of the location coordinated with a 255 isn't changed in any way, so the initial three octets of the IP address (69, 163, 177) will all be coordinated with 255 enabling the first numbers to be gone through. Any number coordinated with 0 is completely counteracted, so the last octet of the location, or 2, would be offset bringing about a 0. So by applying the subnet cover of 255.255.255.0 to the location 69.163.177.2, we find that the system address is 69.163.177.0. In most little systems, a subnet cover of 255.255.255.0 will function admirably, while bigger systems will require an alternate subnet

Kali Linux

veil that may have been determined to give administrations to a particular number of system has.

Kali Linux Default Settings

As clarified before, most entrance test engineers and white hat programmers, won't need their system card to report their essence on the system when the PC associates. This is exactly what Kali Linux will do when it is controlled up and interfaces with a system. Care must be taken when directing an infiltration test to dodge this unneeded additional correspondence by crippling the system card before connecting to the system. With custom introduces including to a hard drive, thumb drive, or SD card, this programmed system design can be changed. Another approach to change this is by building a custom live plate that will be arranged for manual system setup. These techniques will all be examined in Chapter 5 on tweaking Kali Linux.

Utilizing the Graphical User Interface to Configure Network Interfaces

Arranging the system cards, also called system connectors, in Linux was previously a procedure that must be finished through the order line. This has changed as of late, and Kali Linux is the same. Kali Linux has a vigorous graphical UI (GUI) that enables a considerable lot of the basic settings to be designed using straightforward exchange boxes.

The system setups exchange box is effectively open by choosing Applications in the upper right of the UI and afterward choosing

Kali Linux

System Tools, Preferences, and Network associations. By clicking System associations, the System associations discourse box will be shown, and the Wired tab is chosen. On the other hand, right clicking on the two PCs on the upper right of the screen, and choosing Alter Associations will bring about getting to a similar exchange box. Much of the time, PCs will have just one system card that should be arranged, in situations where different NICs are introduced, guaranteeing you are designing the right card. This model will arrange Wired association 1, a name that can be changed if you like to use something increasingly significant, the main physical system card in the PC. The arrangement discourse box is shown subsequent to choosing the association with be changed and clicking the Edit button. This will raise the Editing box for the association, with the Wired tab chosen as a matter of course. This tab shows the gadget's media get to control (MAC) address, a location that is intended to continue as before for the life of the gadget (see the note on MAC addresses for more data on MAC addresses). The gadget's identifier is likewise shown in enclosure after the MAC address. For this situation, the gadget identifier is eth0, where eth is short for Ethernet and 0 is the main card in the PC. The numbering grouping for arrange cards begins at 0 and not 1 so the second card in the PC would be eth1.tab.

Wired Ethernet setups can be made by choosing the 802.1x Security tab, the IPv4 Settings, or the IPv6 Settings tab. This book will concentrate on designing the IP form 4 (IPv4) settings with the goal that tab will be chosen. When chosen the setups for the PCs IP address (192.168.1.66), Subnet Mask or Netmask (255.255.255.0), Gateway (192.168.1.1), and DNS servers

Kali Linux

(192.168.1.1). Various DNS servers can be utilized by isolating each with a comma. The arrangement can be spared and made dynamic by clicking the Save button.

Utilizing The Command Line to Configure Network Interfaces

It is critical to see how to arrange, or reconfigure, the system connector from the direction brief. This is valuable when not utilizing the graphical interface for Linux or in the event that you are associated with a framework remotely through a terminal window. There are various cases in entrance testing where the order line will be the main alternative for making setup changes.

These progressions should be made as a client with raised consents utilizing the root account. It is a decent method to roll out these improvements on a live conveyance and making them using the SDO direction is another alternative for establishments of Kali Linux. When consents have been raised, the system card can be arranged.

Checking the status of the PCs arrange cards and the status of each card is finished with the following order: ifconfig - a

This will show the present arrangement of all system cards on the PC. In Figure 4.7, two system addresses are shown, eth0, the principal Ethernet card and lo, the loopback or inner interface. The settings for this connector were set utilizing the graphical interface. Changing these is basic utilizing the direction brief.

- pag. 182

Kali Linux

Beginning and Stopping the Interface

The interface can be begun using the up choice or halted using the down choice of the ifconfig direction while indicating the interface to be halted or began. The accompanying direction would stop the main Ethernet connector.

The following order would begin the main Ethernet connector.
ifconfig eth0 up

The IP address of this connector can be changed from 192.168.1.66, its present arrangement, to 192.168.1.22 by utilizing the following direction.
ifconfig eth0 192.168.1.22

The order line can be utilized to change the system cover also by utilizing the accompanying direction. This will set the IP address to 192.168.1.22 and set the subnet veil to 255.255.0.0.
ifconfig eth0 192.168.1.22 netmask 255.255.255.0

Full arrangement of the system card at the direction line requires more work than utilizing the graphical UI as the setup settings are not all put away in a similar area. The default door is included or changed, for this situation to 192.168.1.2, with the accompanying direction.

Course include default gw 192.168.1.2

The name server (or DNS) settings are changed by altering the resolv.conf record in the /and so forth index. This can be changed

Kali Linux

by altering the record with your preferred proofreader or basically utilizing the accompanying order at the direction brief.

reverberation nameserver 4.4.4.4. /and so forth/resolv.conf

The above direction will evacuate the current nameserver and supplant it with 4.4.4.4. To include extra nameservers, the accompanying order will annex new nameserver addresses adding to those effectively recorded in resolv.conf.

At the point when the PC plays out a name query, it will check the initial three nameservers in the request they are recorded.

reverberation nameserver 8.8.8.8. /and so on/resolv.conf

DHCP from the Command Prompt

Probably the most effortless approach to design a system card is to utilize DHCP administrations to arrange the card. Along these lines the DHCP server will supply the entirety of the setup settings required for the card. This is helpful for most end clients, however isn't ideal when leading entrance tests as the framework being arranged is signed in the DHCP server's database. Utilize the following directions to incapacitate programmed DHCP setup when leading infiltration tests. This model uses the nano editorial manager; anyway other content tools can be utilized.

nano/and so on/organizing/interfaces

#add the accompanying lines##

auto eth0

Kali Linux

iface eth0 inet static

address {IP_Address}

netmask {netmask}

passage {Gateway_IP_Address}

Spare the content document and exit to finish the adjustment. It might be necessary to bring down and bring back up the Ethernet interfaces to empower this arrangement.

To design the primary system card enter the following direction at the order brief.

dhclient eth0

This will consequently arrange the system card utilizing the settings gave by the DHCP server.

Utilizing The GUI to Configure Wireless Cards

Designing the remote system card can be practiced utilizing the GUI depicted earlier during the graphical setup of the Ethernet interface. For this situation, rather than choosing the tab for Wired, select the Wireless tab in the Network Connections exchange box.

Kali Linux

From this tab select the Add button, which will show an exchange box titled "Altering Wireless association 1" (accepting this is the principal remote connector).

This discourse has four tabs that are used to empower setup of the remote card. This discourse box contains various settings that are utilized to design the framework's remote card.

Association Name

The association name setting defaults to "Remote association" followed by the quantity of the connector being arranged, for this situation Wireless association.

1. This name can be changed to something that is progressively significant, for example, customer 1 remote association.

Associate Automatically Checkbox

When the "Associate naturally" checkbox is chosen, the framework will consequently attempt to interface with the remote system when the PC is begun without client mediation. Like DHCP portrayed before, this might be helpful for most Linux clients. However, it is regularly not the best alternative for the infiltration analyzer as it might declare the analyzer's nearness on the system. If the checkbox is not selected, the analyzer will physically empower the remote connector.

Remote Tab Service Set Identifier

The administration set identifier (SSID) is the system name used to distinguish the remote system. Each system will have a solitary

Kali Linux

SSID that distinguishes the system, and this name will be utilized by customers to associate with the system. In systems with focal passageways, the SSID is determined to the passage and all customers must utilize that SSID to interface with the system. In systems with various passageways, the SSID must be the equivalent on each to empower correspondence.

Mode

The remote card can be designed in two modes either impromptu or foundation. Impromptu systems are regularly casual remote associations between PCs without a focal passageway performing the executive's capacities.

In these associations, every remote association must be arranged to coordinate each other PCs remote settings to set up the association. In foundation mode, focal passages deal with the customers associating with the system and to different PCs in the administration set. All customers must be designed to coordinate the settings characterized in the passageway. The fundamental contrast between these two alternatives is there is no focal organization in specially appointed systems administration while passageways midway oversee associations in framework mode.

Essential Service Set Identification

The essential assistance set identifier (BSSID) is utilized in framework mode to recognize the media to control (MAC) address of the passage. In contrast to the SSID, each passage will have a special BSSID as each ought to have a separate MAC address.

Kali Linux

Gadget MAC Address

The field for the gadget MAC address is utilized to bolt this arrangement to a physical remote connector. This is advantageous when a PC has more than one remote connector. The drop down for this field will be populated with the MAC locations of remote dynamic connectors. Select the right MAC address for the connector you are designing.

Cloned MAC Address

Ordinarily the entrance analyzer won't have any desire to utilize the real MAC address of the connector that is being utilized on the PC. This might be done to sidestep straightforward security strategies, for example, MAC address sifting where just frameworks with explicit MAC delivers are permitted to associate with the system. This should likewise be possible to disguise your remote connector to seem, by all accounts, to be from another maker to coordinate those remote cards being utilized on the remote system.

Most Extreme Transmission Unit

The most extreme transmission unit (MTU) is a systems administration setting that is utilized to decide how huge the systems administration parcels can be to speak with the PC. Much of the time, the MTU can be set to programmed and will work fine. In situations where applications require a particular MTU, read that application's documentation to decide the MTU and set it here.

Remote Security Tab Security Drop Down

- pag. 188

Kali Linux

The Security drop-down zone is utilized to choose the strategy for verifying the remote system. For specially appointed systems, the system clients decide the right security settings, guaranteeing that every customer's security settings coordinate each other's PC in the system. In framework mode, every customer must be arranged to coordinate the security setting of the passageway.

Wired Equivalent Privacy

Wired Equivalent Privacy (WEP) is a more established security technique that utilizes essential encryption innovation to give security identical to wired frameworks. WEP utilizes either a 10 or 26 hexadecimal key to verify the correspondence. The WEP encryption standard has security imperfections that will permit infiltration analyzers to effectively break most WEP encryption keys. Dynamic WEP utilizes port safety efforts illuminated in IEEE 802.1x to give extra safety efforts to the remote system.

Lightweight Extensible Authentication Protocol

Lightweight Extensible Authentication Protocol (LEAP) was created by Cisco Systems to give improved security over the less secure WEP strategy. Jump is like Dynamic WEP.

Wi-Fi Protected Access

Wi-Fi Protected Access (WPA) is an entrance innovation that improves security of remote systems utilizing transient key respectability convention (TKIP) and trustworthiness checks. Systems utilizing WPA are substantially stronger to assaults than WEP-ensured remote systems. The underlying WPA standard was upgraded with the arrival of WPA2 by utilizing a more grounded

Kali Linux

security technique for encryption. In WPA-individual mode, every PC is designed utilizing a key created by a secret word or pass express. WPA undertaking requires a focal Remote Authentication Dial in User Service (RADIUS) server and 802.1x port safety efforts. While WPA venture is convoluted to set up, it gives extra safety efforts.

Passwords and Keys

On the off chance that WEP or WPA individual were chosen as the security technique starting from the drop, type the security key in the secret phrase/key field. Check the Show secret word/key checkbox to confirm the key being utilized has been composed effectively. In situations when the secret word ought not be shown, leave the checkbox unchecked. A few frameworks utilize a strategy for turning passwords or keys. If so, enter the secret word or key for each list by choosing the right list and afterward entering the right key or secret key for that file.

The system may have either open framework or shared key verification. In shared key verification, the passage sends a test instant message to the PC endeavoring to interface. The associating PC at that point scrambles the content with the WEP key and returns the encoded content to the passage.

The passage at that point permits the association if the encryption key utilized by the interfacing PC delivers the right encryption string. Open framework validation then again enables PCs to interface without this test and reaction arrangement, depending on the PC utilizing the right SSID. In the two cases, the

- pag. 190

correspondence channel is finished when the WEP key is utilized to verify the channel. While shared key verification may appear to be increasingly secure, it is in truth less secure as the test message and encoded content reaction are sent in clear content permitting anybody checking the remote channel to catch the test and reaction. As the WEP key is utilized to scramble the test, catching the test and reaction can permit the WEP key to be resolved.

Jump security utilizes the client name and secret word. These should be composed into the suitable fields when LEAP is chosen.

Dynamic WEP and WPA venture require various settings, endorsements, and designs to oversee. These settings won't be covered here; but, if you are joining a system that uses these techniques for security, essentially enter the right subtleties and give the right endorsements.

IPv4 Settings Tab
When the data in Wireless and Wireless Security tabs has been finished, the IPv4 arrangement can be finished. The procedure for designing these settings is the same as the procedure used to arrange the physical Ethernet association depicted earlier.

When the entirety of the necessary data has been given, save the settings by clicking the Save button. After the settings have been saved, the PC will attempt to interface with the system. This is imagined by a realistic in the upper right corner of the screen. Any mistakes will be shown in a discourse box.

Kali Linux

Web Server

Kali Linux contains a simple-to-arrange Apache web server. Having an effectively configurable web server is a huge advantage to the entrance analyzer. For instance, utilizing this administration, sites can be made that copy existing pages on the Internet. These destinations would then be able to be utilized to serve malicious code to clients on the objective system. They will utilize social designing strategies like phishing, including assembling servers facilitating secondary passages, dealing with callbacks, and giving directions to different vindictive programming. There are various different uses the HTTP administration can be put to in an entrance test.

Utilizing the GUI to Start, Stop, or Restart the Apache Server

Utilizing the GUI is the most effortless approach to begin, stop, or restart/reset the web administration. To do this, select Applications from the bar at the highest point of the Kali screen. Starting from the drop down menu select Kali Linux, which will show a submenu. From this menu, select System Administrations, which will thus show another menu; select the HTTP choice on the fly-out menu. This will show the alternatives to begin, stop, and restart the Apache administration.

When a choice is produced using the menu, a direction shell will begin and the status of the server will be shown. Default establishments of Kali Linux will be shown when the Apache server is begun or restarted.

Kali Linux

The blunder you may see is, "Couldn't dependably decide the server's completely qualified area name, utilizing 127.0.0.1 for ServerName." This mistake won't cause any issues now as the web server will be accessible on the system dependent on the framework's IP address. To address this mistake, alter the apache2.conf record in/and so forth/apache2/by adding the server name to be utilized after ServerName toward the finish of this document and afterward spare the record, as pursues.

ServerName localhost

At the point when the Apache server has been begun or restarted, the default site page can be reached by entering the PCs IP address in an internet browser. The Kali Linux circulation incorporates the IceWeasle internet browser that can be reached by clicking on the IceWeasle symbol on the top bar (a blue globe wrapped by a white weasel).

Beginning, Stopping, and Restarting Apache at the Command Prompt

The Apache HTTP server can be effectively begun, halted, and restarted utilizing the order/and so on/init.d/apache2 followed by the activity mentioned (stop, start, or restart). Utilizing the order line brings about indistinguishable activities from the GUI.

/and so on/init.d/apache2 start

/and so forth/init.d/apache2 stop

Kali Linux

/and so forth/init.d/apache2 restart

The Default Web Page

When the Apache administration is ready for action the default (It works!) site page should be changed. To do this, make the web content that ought to be shown on the page and spare it as index.html in the/var/www/catalog. Then again, the current index.html document at this area can be altered and new pages can be included.

FTP Server

The File Transfer Protocol (FTP) is utilized to move documents between PCs. Note that FTP doesn't encode documents or the correspondence channel between PCs so any record navigating the system (or Internet) between the PCs can be seen by anybody observing the system.

Kali Linux does exclude an FTP server so one can be added to encourage moving documents between frameworks. There are various FTP benefits that can be included, one of these is the Pure-FTPd (http://www.pureftpd.org/venture/unadulterated ftpd); notwithstanding, any bolstered FTP daemon ought to be worthy.

Utilize the adept get direction to download and introduce the Pure-FTPd administration using the following order. adept get introduce unadulterated ftpd-basic unadulterated ftpd

- pag. 194

Kali Linux

This will introduce and set up the FTP administration. Some minor setup is important to guarantee appropriate activity of the Pure-FTP Server.

compact disc/and so forth/unadulterated ftpd/conf

reverberation no. Tie

reverberation no. PAMAuthentication

reverberation no. UnixAuthentication

In - s/and so on/unadulterated ftpd/conf/PureDB/and so forth/unadulterated ftpd/auth/50pure

Next gatherings and clients for the FTP administration must be made. First make another framework gathering.

Next include the recently made gathering. This order will give the client no consent to the home index or shell get to.

useradd g ftpgroup - d/dev/invalid s/receptacle/bogus ftpuser

Make a registry for ftp records.

mkdir - p/home/pubftp

Add client envelopes to the ftp registry. For this situation, the client sam that will be made needs an index.

Kali Linux

mkdir/home/pubftp/sam

Now include a client and secret word for the FTP administration. For this situation, the client sam is made.

unadulterated pw useradd sam u ftpuser g ftpgroup d/home/pubftp/sam

A brief will require a secret word be made.

Utilize the following order to refresh the Pure-FTPd database.

unadulterated pw mkdb

At last start the FTP administration with the accompanying direction.

administration unadulterated ftpd start

In the wake of beginning Pure-FTPd, it's a smart thought to test it utilizing the accompanying direction.

ftp {IP_Address}

When indicated enter client name sam and secret phrase. If confirmation was fruitful, the FTP server is working effectively. If this was not effective, reboot the PC and attempt to ftp to the server once more.

Kali Linux

The guide from http://samiux.blogspot.com/2011/08/howto-unadulterated_ftpd-andatftpd-on-backtrack.html was utilized to finish the important strides to make Pure-FTPd practical.

SSH Server

Secure Shell (SSH) is a progressively secure technique for getting to the substance of the Kali Linux record framework from remote areas. SSH gives a protected, encoded interchanges channel between the conveying PCs.

This is useful for infiltration analyzers as it permits record moves to happen without being investigated by organize security devices like interruption identification framework (IDS) and interruption counteractive action framework (IPS).

Produce SSH Keys

To safely utilize SSH, encryption keys must be produced to encourage secure and encoded correspondence. To produce these keys, enter the following at the order brief.

Move the first SSH keys from their default index; don't erase them.

mkdir - p/and so on/ssh/original_keys

mv/and so on/ssh/ssh_host_*/and so on/ssh/original_keys

compact disc/and so on/ssh

- pag. 197

Kali Linux

Create new SSH keys.

dpkg-reconfigure openssh-server

Start/restart the SSH Daemon.

administration ssh (start j restart)

Dealing with the SSH Service from the Kali GUI

The SSH server is incorporated with the primary document structure of the Kali GUI and is gotten to in a similar way that the Apache server is begun or halted. To get to the SSH menu, select Applications from the bar at the highest point of the Kali screen. From the drop down menu that is displayed select Kali Linux. Then select System Services; from the next menu, select the SSH choice on SSH Server 55 the fly-out menu. This will show the choices to begin, stop, and restart the SSH administration.

Dealing with the SSH Server from the Command Line The SSH server can be begun, halted and restarted from here also. Do this after the direction/and so on/init.d/ssh, as outlined in the following directions.

/and so forth/init.d/ssh start

/and so on/init.d/ssh stop

/and so on/init.d/ssh restart

Kali Linux

Getting to the Remote System

When the SSH administration is begun on the Kali framework, the PC can be accessed remotely from Linux frameworks by entering the following direction at the order brief (with a client name of sam and a remote framework IP address of 192.168.1.66).

ssh sam@192.168.1.66

Getting to SSH from a Windows customer will require the utilization of a SSH customer.

A significant number of these are accessible in the Internet; for instance putty is a generally utilized instrument that is accessible from http://putty.org. Introduce the customer and give the IP address or name of the Kali Linux PC as sign in certifications and interface with the remote Kali PC.

Design And Access External Media

Getting to outer media like hard drives or thumb drives is a lot simpler in Kali Linux than in prior adaptations of Backtrack. By and large, media associated with the framework utilizing an all-inclusive sequential transport (USB) connector will be identified and made accessible by the working framework. Nonetheless, if this doesn't occur consequently, physically mounting the drive might be necessary.

Physically Mounting a Drive

The primary thing that must be done when physically mounting a drive to Kali Linux is to interface the physical drive to the PC. Next

Kali Linux

open an order incite and make a mount point. To make the mount point consents for the record being utilized should be raised; this should be possible with the sudo order if the root account isn't being utilized. The accompanying order will make a mount point called newdrive in the media index.

Decide the drive and segment you are interfacing utilizing the fdisk direction with subtleties on the drive you are appending. The primary hard drive will ordinarily be hda, and the main segment on this drive will be hda1. This arrangement proceeds with extra drives associated with the PC with the second being hdb and the third being hdc. More often than not, the essential inside drive will be marked hda so the principal outside drive will be named hdb. To mount the main segment of hdb to the newdrive index made in the last advance use the following order.

mount/dev/hdb1/media/newdrive

When this is finished, the substance of the drive will be accessible by exploring the newdrive index.

compact disc/media/newdrive

Refreshing Kali

Like other working frameworks, Kali has the worked in capacity to refresh both the working framework and the applications, or bundles, introduced. As updates to bundles become accessible, they will be presented on the Kali store. This archive could then be checked to guarantee the working framework and applications are

Kali Linux

cutting-edge. Updates are ordinarily smaller fixes that address programming bugs, or mistakes, or are utilized to include new equipment capacities. Refreshing Kali should be possible with the adept get order line utility. able get update

Redesigning Kali

Like refreshing, redesigning Kali should also be possible at the direction line with the able get utility. Overhauls are ordinarily significant amendments to applications or the working framework itself. Overhauls offer new usefulness and are a lot bigger than updates typically requiring additional existence on the frameworks drive - able get overhaul

Kali Linux

Kali Linux

Chapter 6: Including a Repository Source

As a matter of course Kali checks the product put away in its very own storehouse for updates and redesigns. This is very helpful as certain updates or overhauls could break the usefulness of Kali. Therefore, refreshes and redesigns are tried by the Kali engineers at Offensive Security before they are added to the official Kali store. While this is ordinarily something to be thankful for, there are some product applications that are not accessible when utilizing the default Kali appropriation focuses. Extra storehouses may be included; in this model the Debian archives will be included. Utilizing nano, or an alternate content manager, open/and so on/adept/sources.list.

nano/and so forth/able/sources.list

When open include the accompanying remark and two lines to the base of the record.

#debian 7 principle (this is only a remark)

debhttp://http.us.debian.org/debianstable principle contrib without non

deb-srchttp://http.us.debian.org/debianstable principle contrib without non

- pag. 203

Kali Linux

Presently save the document. In nano this is done by holding down the Control and "O" key to save the record. Save as a similar document name by hitting the Enter key, then use Control and "X" key to exit. This will add the principle Debian vault to the rundown of vaults that Kali will use to check for updates or overhauls and will likewise be utilized to look for applications or bundles to introduce. To settle this change, update Kali with the new archive.

Kali is an amazing asset with a great number of devices introduced as a matter of course. Utilizing a large number of these highlights might be unfamiliar to certain clients, so this part secured huge numbers of the nuts and bolts of successfully utilizing this and numerous other Linux circulations. From arranging system interfaces to adding a FTP server to including another vault and updating the working framework and applications, this section secured a large number of the essential undertakings that must be practiced to viably utilize this toolset. Keeping up Kali is as significant as some other working framework and ought to be done routinely to guarantee its apparatuses, applications and the working framework itself is up to date.

Building A Penetration Testing Lab

Data IN THIS CHAPTER

- Building a Lab

- Metasploitable2

  - pag. 204

Kali Linux

- Extending Your Lab

- The Magical Code Injection Rainbow

Section OVERVIEW AND KEY LEARNING POINTS - This part will clarify step by step instructions to utilize virtualization to fabricate an entrance testing lab establishment and arrangement of VirtualBox establishment of the Metasploitable2 stage in the lab condition.

Before Reading This Chapter: Build A Lab

How does an individual get an opportunity to practice, examine, and become familiar with the misuse procedure? Assemble a lab and take the plunge! Why manufacture a lab when the Internet is readily available? This is a basic inquiry with a considerably more straightforward answer, in light of the fact that nobody needs to go to prison. Imagine the repercussions of testing a system that doesn't belong to you. Assaulting government or monetary frameworks, like a bank, can lead to 20 years or more in a jail.

Obliviousness of laws, either government or state, is no justification with regards to digital wrongdoing. Be cautious, be shrewd, build a lab. The activities in this section are based on freely accessible preparing applications and programming. It is very prudent to construct the lab before moving onto the following part.

Building A Lab On A Dime

- pag. 205

Kali Linux

Prior to the times of virtualization, data innovation (IT) experts, security professionals, and understudies the same had carports, storm cellars, and other rooms brimming with PC gear. At times, these PCs and systems administration hardware were stacked from the floor to the roof and power bills were through the roof. Owning colossal piles of gear was a torment; disregard taking it with you in the event that you needed to move. Be grateful this isn't the situation today.

Regardless of whether your PC is running a Windows, Mac, or Linux working framework, there are two fundamental ways to deal with home virtualization. Both of the accompanying projects cost nothing out of pocket and are accessible for most working frameworks running either a 32-piece or 64-piece design.

VMWare Player
Pros
● Virtual Machines (VMs) are made on a virtual switch committed for NAT.

Numerous VMs will have the option to speak with one another, and access from the host machine is conceivable.

● A DHCP is introduced as a matter of course, and all VMs can get IP addresses consequently.

● Advanced virtualization support for Xen, XenServer, vSphere, and other major hypervisors.

Kali Linux

Cons

● Not accessible for Mac, Solaris, or FreeBSD working frameworks.

● Does not take into consideration taking depictions or cloning of existing VMs.

● Difficulties with some Wi-Fi organize connectors.

VirtualBox

Pros

● Available for Windows, Linux, Mac, Solaris, and FreeBSD.

● Functions are accessible to clone VMs (spares time).

● Supports increasingly virtual hard plate record types. This is particularly helpful when **running downloaded and prebuilt VMs.**

Cons

● VMs are disengaged from one another except if port sending is empowered on the host.

Kali Linux

● Does not bolster propelled virtualization required for Xen, XenServer, vSphere, or different kinds of hypervisors.

● If the VM crashes, there is a higher probability that the whole VM will get defiled.

This guide is explicitly for Oracle's VirtualBox adaptation 4.2.16 introduced on Microsoft Windows 7 Professional. The choice was made to utilize VirtualBox rather than VMWare Player because there are more assets accessible on the Internet to help if issues emerge; nonetheless, it requires some additional arrangement.

Keep in mind, the best examination is your investigation while picking a virtualization framework. There has been quite a discussion over which is the best, eventually picking one virtualization framework over another is an individual inclination. Likewise, not at all like antivirus programs, both can be introduced to encourage different needs, so it is conceivable to introduce VirtualBox and VMWare Player on a similar PC. The connections and references utilized all through this guide were accessible at the time of writing. Know that renditions, download areas, and data may change at any time.

Introducing VirtualBox on Microsoft Windows 7

Open an internet browser and explore to: https://www.virtualbox.org/wiki/DOWNLOADS

Kali Linux

It is important to ensure the web address is entered accurately.

Select the right form of the program for your working framework and start the download procedure. After the download is finished, run the executable. Figure outlines the welcome discourse box for the VirtualBox establishment. Click on Next to proceed.

This instructional exercise won't cover custom arrangement or propelled establishments. Acknowledge the default alternatives in the exchange box showed, and click Next to proceed.

Establishment

1. Pick your symbol settings as represented in Figure 5.3, and click Next. A system association caution will show up, click Yes to continue.

2. Click the Introduce button. If the Microsoft client account control (UAC) window shows up, click Yes to proceed.

3. The establishment may incite the client to introduce gadget drivers as shown in Figure 5.6. Click Install to proceed with when prompted. (This may happen a few times.)

After the establishment finishes, click the Finish button.

The VirtualBox establishment is currently finished and if the "Start Oracle VM VirtualBox 4.2.16 after establishment" setting was

Kali Linux

checked, VirtualBox will open showing the VirtualBox Manager. No virtual machines will be made right now so the administrator can be shut.

Open an internet browser and go back to: https://www.virtualbox.org/wiki/Downloads. Download the VirtualBox 4.2.16 Oracle VM VirtualBox Extension Pack. When downloaded, double click the document to execute it.

Click Install to proceed. Consent to the End User License Agreement when prompted. If the Windows UAC exchange box shows up, click Yes to proceed. Close out VirtualBox when the establishment is finished.

Setting Up a Virtual Attack Platform

To keep everything in a virtualized lab, it's a smart thought to make a VM that can run Kali Linux. The steps below depict how to set up Kali Linux to run as a live boot framework inside VirtualBox. When the VM has been made and propelled, a hard drive establishment as depicted in Chapter 2 can be performed. It is necessary to have a virtual machine devoted to propelling live boot pictures. While trying out frameworks or modifying ISOs, this live boot virtual machine can be utilized again and again with little change to the design.

Set Up a Virtual Machine for Kali Linux in VirtualBox

Open VirtualBox, and click on New.

Making a VM

- pag. 210

Kali Linux

1. Give the new virtual machine a name, for this situation Kali-Linux-LiveDisc was utilized. Set the sort to: Linux, set the variant to: Debian or Debian (64 piece) as pertinent, and click Next to proceed.

2. This stage will run only in the virtual machines RAM. Make a point to set the RAM size to at least 2 GB. 4 GB is prescribed; more is better if accessible.

3. Click Next to proceed. Next select the "Make a virtual hard drive now" alternative, and click Create to proceed.

4. Select the VMDK (Virtual Machine Disk) alternative, and click Next to proceed.

5. Select the Fixed Size alternative, and click Next.

6. The default name and hard drive size will be okay a live plate situation; in any case, if you want to make a full establishment of Kali Linux in VirtualBox, change the virtual hard drive size to 40 GB. Click Create to proceed.

a. Try not to control on the machine when the procedure is finished.

7. Select the Kali-Linux-LiveDisc virtual machine, and afterward click the Settings button. Select the General catch from the menu on the left and explore to the Advanced tab. Set the Shared

Kali Linux

Clipboard setting to: Bidirectional, and set the Drag'n'Drop setting to: Bidirectional.

8. Select the Storage button from the menu on the left. Click on the Controller: IDE "Disc" symbol set apart as Empty. Spot a check mark in the Live CD/DVD alternative on the correct side of the window. Explore to the downloaded ISO record for Kali Linux.

9. Select the Network button from the menu on the left and change the Attached to: Host-just Adapter.

10. Click OK to save changes, and return to the primary screen.

Building the Kali Linux virtual machine is finished.

Kali Linux

Chapter 7: Metasploitable

Quick has pre-customized a PC that has various security openings and is deliberately defenseless. This is an incredible instrument to begin PC security preparing, yet it's not prescribed as a base working framework. The VM will give the analyst numerous chances to learn entrance testing with the Metasploit Framework. Metasploitable2
is a virtual machine that comes pre-worked for accommodation and simple to use. This is likewise a decent beginning stage for building a virtualized lab in light of the fact that a significant number of the applications that are talked about further in this section can be introduced over the Metasploitable2 VM.

Introducing Metasploitable2

Open an internet browser and visit: http://sourceforge.net/. Use the inquiry bar to look for Metasploitable. In the outcomes, click on the connection for Metasploitable2. Click on Download to get the VM.

Save the download to an area that will be recollected. If not effectively open, dispatch VirtualBox.

Click the New button to make a VM.

1. Name the virtual machine Metasploitable2 and set the Type to: Linux. Set the Version to Ubuntu, and click Next to proceed.

Kali Linux

2. (Outside of the Wizard) Extract the substance of the Metasploitable2.zip holder to: C:/clients/%USERNAME%/VirtualBoxVMs/ Metasploitable2/. (Back to the VirtualBox Wizard) Set the memory size for the virtual machine. Click Next to proceed. 512 MB of RAM ought to be satisfactory; the size can be changed if essential.

Select the spiral button "Utilize a current virtual hard drive document." Use the Browse catch to choose: c:/clients/%USERNAME%/VirtualBox VMs/Metasploitable2/Metasploitable.vmdk record.

Click Create to proceed; DO NOT dispatch the virtual machine now.

Select the virtual machine, and afterward click on the Settings button. Click on General from the menu on the left. Then select the Advanced tab.

Set the Shared Clipboard setting to: Bidirectional, and set the Drag'n'Drop setting to: Bidirectional. Select the Network button from the Menu on the left and change the Attached to: Host-just Adapter. Click OK to save the changes.

Select the Metasploitable2 virtual machine, and click on the Start button at the top.

Sign into Metasploitable2 with the default qualifications:

- pag. 215

Kali Linux

Username: msfadmin

Secret phrase: msfadmin

First thing to note is that there is no GUI as a matter of course. Metasploitable isn't intended to be utilized as an assault stage. The purpose of signing into Metasploitable as of now is to confirm its usefulness and decide its IP address so it very well may be assaulted by Kali Linux later.

Check the IP address that was relegated to your virtual machine.

a. Type: ifconfig

b. As a matter of course VirtualBox's DHCP server rents out IP tends to beginning with 192.168.56.x.

:Presumption: 192.168.56.101

Dispatch the Kali-Linux-LiveDisc virtual machine that was made before. Subsequent to signing into Kali, open IceWeasel (the default internet browser in Kali) and explore to the IP address for the Metasploitable2 virtual machine.

Expanding Your Lab

With the Metasploitable2 Project, the learner doesn't simply get a powerless machine to assault, but a portal into different regions of preparing. The virtual machine itself is defenseless against remote

Kali Linux

and nearby adventures commonly; the accompanying web administrations accompany Metasploitable.

1. phpMyAdmin—Managing SQL through a web interface is rarely simple, however phpMyAdmin is a free web application written in PHP detail which improves the organization of MySQL databases associating with web servers. Direct access to MySQL database is conceivable through phpMyAdmin and along these lines a succulent objective for pentester and programmers.

More Information: http://www.phpmyadmin.net/.

2. Mutillidae (articulated mut-till-I-day) is an open source anticipated from OWASP that is devoted to helping security specialists and understudies in creating web application hacking aptitudes. Mutillidae is an very helpful preparing apparatus with huge network support and is refreshed all the time. It comes introduced of course on Metasploitable2, SamuraiWTF, and OWASP Broken Web Apps (BWA).

Numerous instructional exercise recordings for Mutillidae have been transferred to YouTube by Jeremy Drunin, otherwise called webpwnized in the security network. The rendition that drops naturally with Metasploitable is obsolete and lacking more current difficulties. Download the most recent form of Mutillidae from the Sourgeforge venture page and transfer it to the/var/www envelope in Metasploitable2 to get the most recent updates.

More Information:

Kali Linux

http://sourceforge.net/ventures/mutillidae/;
http:/www.youtube.com/client/webpwnized.

3. WebDAV—Website administrators and chairmen may need to make changes to the substance of sites. WebDAV is an expansion to the HTTP convention suite enabling changes to sites remotely. WebDAV utilizes a username and password blend to manage account access. If the WebDAV setting isn't verified, assailants might mutilate sites, transfer noxious records, and utilize the web server for different wicked goals. More Information: http://www.webdav.org/.

4. DVWA—Damn Vulnerable Web App is another preparation stage for security experts, educators, understudies, and analysts for finding out about web application security, and as the name suggests, it's damn defenseless. More Information: http://www.dvwa.co.uk http://sourceforge.net/ventures/dvwa.

5. TWiki—An undertaking level, web 2.0 application wiki and coordinated effort web frontend. TWiki is strong and has had numerous variants that have turned out after the one in Metasploitable. The quantity of vulnerabilities in the introduced form on the Metasploitable virtual machine is amazing. TWiki will give a pentester a more noteworthy point of view on the quantity of approaches to assault web 2.0 applications. More current renditions of TWiki have been utilized by corporate mammoths, for example, Yahoo!, Nokia, Motorola, and Disney. More Information: http://twiki.org.

- pag. 218

Kali Linux

The entirety of the applications above are overhauled on an Apache Tomcat webserver. Any organizer or site that is put in the/var/www envelope will be available through the web interface on the Metasploitable2 virtual machine. There are many preparing bundles like Mutillidae and DVWA that will help sharpen and hone a pentester's ranges of abilities. Besides, these preparation programs still get refreshes; Metasploitable was never intended to be refreshed between significant discharges. Including bundles onto the Metasploitable virtual machine takes time, however the exertion is well justified, despite all the trouble. As a repeatable model, change the accompanying strides to add bundles to the Metasploitable virtual machine's web administrations.

The Magical Code Injection Rainbow

Dan Crowley, a data security lover and free scientist with Trustwave, has structured and generated five noteworthy preparing suites. His electronic preparing programs are easy to explore and accompanied different testing levels. His most recent creation is a blend of his web coaches pounded into one advanced play area called, the Magical Code Injection Rainbow (MCIR). MCIR contains the following modules:

- SQLol—a SQL infusion preparing stage that takes into consideration customization of white and boycotted characters and successions concentrated on a test-based stage to prepare the essential aptitudes important to test and thrashing SQL safety efforts.

Kali Linux

- XMLmao—Similar to SQLol, XMLmao is a configurable XML infusion preparing condition.

- Shelol—A configurable working framework shell preparing condition for direction infusion.

- XSSmh—Corss-site scripting preparing device.

- CryptOMG—as co-venture with Andrew Jordan, CryptOMG is a configurable catch the banner style web application intended to misuse basic blemishes in the usage of cryptography. More Information: https://github.com/SpiderLabs/MCIR.

Establishment of MCIR

Open VirtualBox, select the Metasploitable2 virtual machine, and click the Settings button from the menu bar (this should even be possible while the machine is at present running). Select the Network button on the left and change the Attached to setting to: Bridged Adapter.

The Name setting is the system card that the virtual system interface card is to be appended to. Singular outcomes may contrast. Click the OK button to give in and close the window. If

Kali Linux

not already done, dispatch the Metasploitable2 virtual machine and sign in as the msfadmin client. Reset the system interface.

sudo ifdown eth0

sudo ifup eth0

Check to guarantee the new IP address has been set.

ifconfig eth0

Change the nameservers in/and so on/resolve.conf.

sudo nano/and so forth/resolve.conf

Change the IP address of the name server inclined to an open entryway on your system; at that point press CTRL 1 X to exit, and save the record.

Test for Internet availability.

nslookupwww.google.com

The entirety of the IP addresses for Google.com will be shown. If not, return and modify the system interface settings.

Download the Magical Code Injection Review from GitHub.com. https://codeload.github.com/SpiderLabs/MCIR/zip/ace

- pag. 221

Kali Linux

The document downloaded doesn't have a "zip" expansion; notwithstanding, it is a ZIP holder that will be downloaded from GitHub.com.

Uncompress the ace document.

unfasten ace

Move the MCIR organizer into place on the Tomcat web server.
sudo mv MCIR-ace/var/www/mcir

Alter the Metasploitable2 site page for simpler openness.

compact disc/var/www

sudo nano index.php

Add the MCIR to the rundown on the site page.

Press CTRL 1 X to exit and save the record. The MCIR structure isn't totally stacked. The system settings must be turned around. Open the VirtualBox chief window, select the Metasploitable2 virtual machine, and snap on the Settings button from the menu bar. As in the past, select the Network button from the menu on the left and change the Attached to setting to: Host-just Adapter. Click OK to save and exit. Then reset the system interface card on the Metasploitable2 virtual machine.

sudo ifdown eth0

- pag. 222

Kali Linux

sudo ifup eth0

Check the new IP address on the eth0 organize interface card.

ifconfig eth0

From the Kali-Linux-LiveDisc virtual machine, open IceWeasel, and explore to: http://{ip address of Metasploitable2 virtual machine}/.

The MCIR connect is accessible through the internet browser.

Utilize this strategy for refreshing and including new substance into the Metasploitable2 virtual machine. Later this book will talk about how to utilize the Metasploit Framework to abuse this virtual machine.

Prologue to the Penetration

Test Lifecycle

Data IN THIS CHAPTER

- Reconnaissance

- Scanning

- Exploitation

Kali Linux

- Maintaining Access

- Reporting

Section OVERVIEW AND KEY LEARNING POINTS - This part will present the five periods of the entrance testing life cycle

Prologue To The Lifecycle

The vast majority of people expect that all that an entrance analyzer, or programmer, needs to do is plunk down before a PC and start composing a dark string of code and, voila, any PC on the planet is in a flash opened. This generalization situated in Hollywood legend is a long way from reality. Experts in this field are extremely fastidious in the methodology utilized when revealing and misusing vulnerabilities in PC frameworks. After some time a demonstrated structure has developed that is utilized by proficient moral programmers. The four periods of this structure direct the infiltration analyzer through the procedure of experimentally misusing data frameworks, so that outcomes in a well-recorded report that can be utilized if necessary to rehash bits of the testing commitment. This procedure gives a structure to the analyzer as well as growing significant level designs for entrance testing exercises. Each stage expands on the past advance and gives detail to the progression that pursues. While the procedure is consecutive, numerous analyzers come back to previous stages to explain revelations and approve discoveries.

The initial four stages in the process have been characterized by Patrick Engebretson in his book *The Basics of Hacking and*

Kali Linux

Penetration Testing. These means are Reconnaissance, Scanning, Exploitation, and Maintaining Access.

This book utilizes these advances, but extends Patrick's work with an extra advance: Reporting. Also, when contrasted with the five-stage process characterized by EC-Council in its well-known Certified Ethical Hacking (CjEH) course, many may see the last period of that procedure, Covering Tracks, is absent. This was done deliberately to concentrate on the prior stages and remember a part for detailing, a theme that is overlooked from numerous books on this subject. This book likewise separates from the prior book by evacuating the cyclic representation of the existence cycle and supplanting it with an increasingly direct perception delineation that matches what a moral programmer would typically experience in an ordinary commitment. This would start with surveillance of the objective data framework. It ends with the infiltration analyzer or test group captain instructs the data frameworks authority and reports on what was found.

An essential perspective on every one of the eliminates will be in this part and an increasingly broad depiction will be made in the sections dedicated to each stage. Notwithstanding the depiction regular devices for each stage will be presented in the coming parts.

The infiltration testing life-cycle.
Section 6: Introduction to the Penetration Test Life cycle shows the periods of the lifecycle. Additionally, it has a view in the engine of what apparatuses are well on the way to be utilized first by

Kali Linux

engineers in this field of security. These sections will acquaint the user with the instruments; however, it won't be comprehensive, but will start to expose what each apparatus or strategy can do to help with leading these kinds of tests. Huge numbers of the instruments or systems have whole books—sometimes numerous books—dedicated to their right use and application.

Stage 1: RECONNAISSANCE

In a little room with dim lights, experts and officials check and review maps of a threatening area. Over the room others stare at the TV slots over the globe hysterically taking notes. The last gathering in this room readies a nitty gritty evaluation of everything about the objective being examined. While this situation shows what might regularly be done in a military observation of a potential objective, it is similar to what the entrance analyzer will do during the surveillance period of the infiltration testing life cycle.

This stage centers around getting the hang of everything about the system and association that is the objective of the commitment.

This is finished via looking through the Internet and leading latent sweeps of the accessible associations with the objectives arrange. In this stage, the analyzer doesn't really enter the system guards yet, rather distinguishes and reports however much data session the objective as could be expected.

Stage 2: SCANNING

Kali Linux

Behind enemy lines, a solitary trooper is tucked away among a shrubbery of hedges and trees. The report being sent back advises others about the area regarding the camp being watched, and the sorts of work that is being done in each building. The report likewise takes note of the courses all through the camp and sorts of security that can be seen.

The trooper in this model had a strategic objective by the examination led during the observation stage. This is valid for the second period of the entrance testing life cycle. The analyzer will utilize data picked up in stage 1 to begin really filtering the objectives system and data framework. Utilizing apparatuses in this stage, a superior meaning of the system and framework foundation of the data framework will be focused for abuse. The data picked up in this stage will be utilized in the abuse stage.

Stage 3: EXPLOITATION

Four officers race through an open field; the moon is just a sliver and darkened by mists, but the fighters see everything in a ghostly green gleam. They surge the structure sneaking past a hole in the fence and afterward through an open indirect access. After only minutes on the objective they are headed out with fundamental data about future troop developments and plans for the coming months.

Again this matches what the moral programmer will do in the abuse stage. The plan of this stage is to get into the objective

Kali Linux

framework and secretly exit with data, utilizing framework vulnerabilities and demonstrated systems.

Stage 4: MAINTAINING ACCESS

In view of drawings gave by the assault group, a gathering of gifted architects unearth from somewhere down in the tree line the room that held the imperative data taken before. The reason for this passage is to give simple access to the space for abuse of the adversary. This is the equivalent for the analyzer, when the framework is misused for indirect accesses and rootkits are left on the frameworks to permit later access.

Stage 5: REPORTING

The strike group officer remains before a gathering of commanders and chief naval officers clarifying the subtleties of the assault. Each progression is clarified in incredible detail developing each detail that enabled the misuse to occur. The entrance analyzer too should create nitty gritty reports to clarify each progression in the hacking procedure, vulnerabilities abused, and frameworks that were really undermined. Moreover, as a rule, one individual from the group, and sometimes more, might be required to give a point by point preparation to senior initiative and specialized staff of the objective data framework.

Outline

- pag. 228

Kali Linux

The coming sections will clarify every one of these stages in more detail. Every part will give data on the rudiments of the regular devices utilized for each stage. Utilizing the procedure nitty gritty in the user will comprehend the reason and preferences of stage being clarified and the most widely recognized instruments utilized in that stage.

Surveillance

Data IN THIS CHAPTER

- Website Mirroring

- Google Searches

- Google Hacking

- Social Media

- Job Sites

- DNS and DNS Attacks

Part OVERVIEW AND KEY LEARNING POINTS - This section will clarify the rudiments of the observation period of the entrance testing life-cycle. This procedure will enable the moral programmer to find data about the objective association and PC frameworks, which can be utilized later in connecting with the PC frameworks.

Kali Linux

Presentation

Similarly as military organizers intently dissect the accessible data before creating battle designs, a fruitful entrance analyzer should intently break down the entirety of the data that can be acquired before directing an effective infiltration test. Commonly this data can be picked up via looking through the Internet utilizing Internet locales like Google and others including those that are centered around data sharing and online life. Data can be found on the Internet's name servers that give guidance to client's programs also. Email messages can be followed through an association and even returned email can help the entrance analyzer.

Making and analyzing a disconnected duplicate of the objective site can give a wellspring of significant data and can be utilized later as a device for social building undertakings, whenever permitted by the tests ROE.

This stage begins with the test group thinking minimally about the objective. The degree of detail given to the group can run from knowing just the association's name and maybe a site address to itemized and explicit framework data including IP address space and innovations utilized characterized in the ROE to restrict or scope the test occasion. The ROE may likewise confine the test group's capacity to lead exercises remembering bans on social building and ruinous exercises like forswearing of administration (DoS) and appropriated refusal of administration (DDoS) assaults.

Kali Linux

The objective is to discover a lot of data you can about the association.

A few things that ought to be resolved about the association include:

hierarchical structure including point by point elevated level, departmental, and group authoritative outlines;

hierarchical foundation including IP space and system topology;

advancements utilized including equipment stages and programming bundles;

representative email addresses;

authoritative accomplices;

physical areas of the authoritative offices;

telephone numbers.

Confided in Agents

The believed specialist might be the individual that employed the entrance test group or a person that was assigned by the association that will have the option to respond to inquiries regarding the commitment. That person won't uncover the way that an infiltration test is jumping out at the association.

- pag. 231

Chapter 8: Start with the Target's Own Website

The objective's claim site holds immense data for building up the profile for the commitment. For instance, numerous locales gladly show authoritative outlines and key pioneer's profiles. These ought to be utilized as a reason for building up an objective profile and data about key pioneers in the association. They can be utilized for further reaping of data via web-based networking media locales and for social building, whenever permitted in the expressed ROE.

Numerous authoritative sites likewise incorporate a job openings page. This page can be basic in deciding the advancements utilized in the association. For instance, postings for frameworks chairmen that know about Active Directory and Windows Server 2012 would be a solid marker that the association is in any event utilizing Windows Server 2012. A similar posting for head's recognizable or master in the organization of Windows Server 2003 or 2000 should make any infiltration analyzer's ears perk up as these stages are powerless compared to more up to date working frameworks.

Each webpage ought to be checked for a connect to web mail and whenever discovered it ought to be assessed. On the off chance that clicking the connection shows an Outlook Web Access page, it would be a decent supposition that Microsoft Exchange servers are being utilized for email. In the event that an Office 365 page is shown, it is a decent pointer that email administrations are being re-appropriated and the mail servers would likely be too far out dependent on most ROEs. This would be valid for Google web mail

Kali Linux

too; be that as it may, this should all be point by point in the limits characterized before the commitment started. If inquiries on the plausibility of intersection a limit exist, the commitment believed operator ought to be utilized to determine the inquiry.

Site Mirroring

There are times it is increasingly compelling to duplicate the association's whole site to assess when disconnected. This could be to utilize robotized apparatuses to scan for terms or just to have a duplicate on the off chance that changes ought to be made to delicate data that is on the present site. It is valuable just to have a duplicate of the site to proceed with surveillance when disconnected. Instruments like the direction line wget will duplicate the entirety of the html records from a site and store them on the neighborhood hard drive. The instrument wget is introduced in Kali Linux and is a straightforward device to utilize. By using the following direction line in the terminal window, the html records from a whole site will be downloaded. It is imperative to take note that wget won't duplicate server-side programming for pages, for example, those made with a PHP content.

wget m p E K np - v http://foo.com

In this model, the wget direction is trailed by various switches or alternatives. As with the devices on Kali Linux, the client manual can be referenced to decide the wagers utilization of the apparatus for the commitment being led. To see the wget man pages, utilize the accompanying order. man wget

- pag. 233

Kali Linux

Once in the man pages, survey the substance by utilizing the here and there bolts and the page up and page down catches. Press the h key for help and press q to leave the man pages. An audit of the wget man pages for this arrangement of switches uncovers the following:

- m reflect, turn on choices that are appropriate for reflecting the site;

- p page or essentials, this alternative guarantees required documents are downloaded including pictures and css records;

- E alter expansion, this will make all pages be saved locally as a html document;

- k convert interfaces, this empowers the documents to be changed over for nearby review;

- K keep reinforcement changed over, will back up the first document with a.orig postfix.

The documents moved from an association's web servers will be put away in an envelope with the name of the site that was replicated. When duplicating a site, mistakes may happen when pages made with or containing PHP are downloaded. This is

Kali Linux

because much code to make the page is made by a content that sudden spikes in demand for the server behind the site page in an area that most site cloning applications can't get to.

When the records are downloaded, it is significant that they are not made accessible for review by others, for example, reposting the site as this would establish an infringement of copyright law.

Google Searches

The hunt Google method uses the propelled administrators used to direct point by point look with Google. Those new to looking with Google can begin with the Google Advance Search page situated at http://www.google.com/advanced_search. This page will help walk amateur searchers through essential ventures. The top portion of the page will assist finding web pages by including and barring words and numbers. The bottom portion of the page will help thin the outcomes utilizing Google's administrators. The searcher can utilize any blend of fields on this page to build the pursuit string that will be utilized. Utilizing more than one field will make an increasingly unpredictable, but progressively engaged inquiry string.

Every One of These Words

This field can be utilized to discover pages containing the words composed in the exchange box paying little mind to where they are on the website page. The words don't need to be in the request composed or together, only some place on the page. To lead this inquiry, type various terms in the discourse box and click the Advanced Search Button. By doing this the words composed in the

Kali Linux

development search page are converted into an inquiry string, and afterward sent to Google as though they were composed straightforwardly in the pursuit field on the principle Google page.

This Exact Word or Phrase

Composing an inquiry term in the field to one side of this choice will cause the Google web search tool to discover the words or expression in the precise request composed. Dissimilar to the "every one of these words" search, only website pages that contain the expression or words in the accurate request and together will be remembered for the outcome set. This inquiry works by setting the hunt terms inside statements.

Any of These Words

When utilizing this field Google search will discover pages that contain any of the words. Not at all like the "every one of these words" field, the pages returned don't have the entirety of the words that were composed. This hunt works by putting the OR connector between terms in the inquiry box.

None of These Words

The words composed in this content box will be utilized to preclude pages from the subsequent Google search. Any pages containing the words composed will be expelled from the outcome set. This pursuit works by putting a short sign before the words or terms you don't need in the outcome set.

Numbers Ranging from

Kali Linux

By utilizing the two content fields here the hunt will discover pages that have numbers that in the range composed. This kind of search can be upgraded by including units of measure, for example, pound (lb), miles, or millimeters (mm) or cash like $. This inquiry can be directed in the principal search box by setting two periods between the numbers.

Language

By choosing a language starting from the drop selector, the subsequent pages will for the most part be in the language chosen. This inquiry restrictor can be useful to limit results to pages that are written in the language generally predominant in the region that the objective is situated. For instance, by concentrating on German sites, a group leading an infiltration test on a German firm can all the more likely look for data important to this specific commitment.

Locale

By choosing a locale, starting from the drop selector, the subsequent pages will be from site pages distributed in the area chosen. If no choice is produced using the dialects drop down, the outcomes from a hunt with an area chosen will incorporate pages distributed in that locale, paying little respect to the essential language utilized. By choosing both a language and area, a progressively engaged pursuit can be directed.

Last Updated

By choosing a period limit in the drop down menu, just pages refreshed inside the chosen time span will be remembered. This

Kali Linux

will guarantee more established pages are excluded from the outcome set and can be utilized to ensure the subsequent pages are after a key occasion. For instance, if the association that is the focal point of the infiltration test as of late finished a merger with another association or received another innovation, the search could be restricted to the time since the occasion to guarantee the query items are increasingly applicable.

Site or Domain

This content box can be one of the most supportive when narrowing list items on the objective. For instance, looking for an administration association may profit by confining the outcomes to only .gov spaces, while looking on Foo Incorporated may profit by restricting outcomes to the foo.com area. This kind of limitation can likewise be led in the fundamental Google search content box by utilizing the hunt restrictor site, trailed by the area or spaces that ought to be returned in the outcomes set. For instance, use site: foo.com to confine results to just pages from the foo.com area.

Terms Appearing

By utilizing this drop down the search question can be focused at a particular piece of the page. Clearly choosing "anyplace on the page" would run the search on whole pages of Internet destinations with no genuine limitations on where the inquiry question was focused.

A search on utilizing "in title of the page" will just focus on the title of website pages.

- pag. 238

Kali Linux

To be explicit, the title of the page is the piece of the website page that is shown in the tabs of the internet browser. This inquiry can likewise be led on the primary Google page by utilizing the intitle: administrator in the search box.

Utilizing the limiter "in the content of the page" will confine the pursuit to just the content of the page. It will prohibit things like pictures, records, and page structure like the title. If these things are written in the content of the page, the inquiry will restore these things in the outcomes. For instance, if a picture is referenced in the content of the page, that picture will be returned in the indexed lists; this is valid for picture markup and connections in content also. Utilizing the intext: administrator in the Google search box is equal to choosing this choice from the drop down.

Utilizing the "in URL of the page" will limit searches to the page uniform resource locator (URL). The URL is the location of the site page that shows up in the location box of the internet browser. At last, utilizing the "in connections to the page" will discover pages that connect to the inquiry criteria. This pursuit can be led in the primary Google search box by utilizing the inurl: administrator.

Safe Search
Safe inquiry has two alternatives: "show most important outcomes" and "channel unequivocal." The channel express setting can lessen explicitly express recordings and pictures from the indexed lists. Choosing the show most important outcomes won't channel the outcomes for explicitly unequivocal substance.

- pag. 239

Kali Linux

Understanding Level

The perusing level choice will channel results by the multifaceted nature of the content in the website pages that will be come back from the hunt. The "no perusing level showed" will execute the pursuit with no perusing level channel applied. The choice "explain results with understanding level" will show all outcomes; the perusing level of each page will be shown in the indexed lists. The Google calculation isn't as logical or fine-grained as other evaluation level understanding instruments, including the Lexile level. However, it is very productive in separating results into these three classes; essential, middle, and progressed. This can be accommodating when leading an infiltration test by concentrating the outcomes on the perusing level of the objective. For instance, look on a logical association could be restricted to those pages with a propelled understanding level. Attempting every one of the three levels may be useful to see distinctive indexed lists and significant data can be picked up from look through utilizing the essential understanding level.

Record Type

Record type can be one of the most significant hunts that an infiltration analyzer can utilize. This setting contains the list items to a particular record type, for example, .doc and .docx for Microsoft Word Documents of .pdf for Adobe archives. Ordinarily clients will utilize distinctive record types for various kinds of data. Common client names, passwords, and different sorts of record data will be put away in spreadsheets with .xls or .xlsx expansions.

Kali Linux

The drop down offers a large number of the most widely recognized record types and any augmentation can be utilized in the Basic Google search box by utilizing the filetype: administrator, e.g., filetype:xls.

Utilization Rights

Utilization rights constrains the query items by the capacity to reuse the substance dependent on copyright and other reuse confinements. By choosing "Allowed to utilize, share, or change," the outcomes returned will be content that can be reused with confinements that stipulate how it can be reused. For example, the substance can't be altered, for the most part without a charge. Allowed to utilize, offer, or adjust will return in the list items that have pages that can be altered inside the permit limitations. The outcomes will enable the content to be redistributed regularly without an expense. The alternatives with the term business in the choice work as those without the term business, however, return results that can be utilized industrially.

Aggregating an Advanced Google Search

Utilizing the fields exclusively on the Google propelled page restores some noteworthy indexed lists, yet utilizing a large number of these fields together will improve the manner in which an entrance analyzer finds significant data. For instance, accept that Foo International (an American Company) merged with another organization a month back and mentioned an entrance test from your group. In the midst of progress like this, numerous archives are made to help individuals from each organization in the change; it might be conceivable that a representative presented hierarchical graphs on the organization's site. One potential search could utilize the accompanying fields and terms: authoritative graph

language: English

district: United States

last update: past month

site or space: foo.com

document type: pdf.

The outcomes could then be additionally refined by including or expelling search fields or changing the alternatives. For instance, changing the record type to PowerPoint (.ppt) or evacuating the document type out and out may restore the outcomes required.

Google Hacking

Google Hacking is a method that was spearheaded by Johnny Long and utilizes explicit Google administrators and terms in Internet searches to return significant data utilizing the Google web crawler.

This strategy centers around utilizing explicitly focused on articulations to search the Google databases for data about individuals and associations.

Kali Linux

This procedure takes the Google look through portrayed before and supercharges their outcomes.

Google Hacking utilizes propelled administrators and connected choices to make focused on questions that can be run in the Google web crawler. Commonly the ventures will be focused at gathering data about explicit advancements, like board administrations and other searches will target client certifications. A few incredible books have been composed that completely clarify Google Hacking, the most popular being *Google Hacking for Penetration Testers* composed by Johnny Long and distributed by Syngress.

Google Hacking Database

An incredible number of Google Hacking search question strings have been assembled into the Google Hacking Database (GHDB). The first database is situated at http://www.hackersforcharity.org/ghdb/, Offensive Security likewise has a GHDB at http://www.offensive-security.com/network ventures/google-hacking-database/ that develops the first database, and begets the expression "Googledorks," a moniker for bumbling or stupid individuals as uncovered by Google. At the time of writing, the GHDB, kept up by Offensive Security, contained more than 3350 Google Hacks isolated into 14 classifications. More than 160 of these quest strings can be useful for discovering documents that contain passwords. A case of one of these inquiry strings that would endeavor to discover Cisco passwords is represented below. empower secret phrase j mystery "current arrangement" - intext:the

- pag. 243

Kali Linux

Running this search returned nearly a million and a half destinations. Keeping in mind that a portion of the records returned may not contain real passwords, an extraordinary number of the outcomes really contained secret word records. This search could be additionally refined to address the issues of individual infiltration tests by including extra administrators, for example, the site or space administrator as searches.

Web Based Life

Web based life has become an incorporated piece of numerous individual's everyday lives. This reality makes online networking a treasure trove for social affair data in this period of the entrance testing life cycle. Data that is secured by individuals in the physical world is posted unreservedly by those same individuals via web-based networking media locales. Utilizing destinations like Facebook, Instagram, Twitter, LinkedIn, among others, a full profile of people working at the objective area can be created. This can help in social designing commitment.

LinkedIn is especially useful in creating hierarchical diagrams. Worked for associating experts, LinkedIn will regularly fill in clear spots on the objective profile, including a superior characterized hierarchical outline and even email address records. This is despite the fact that this last advance will frequently require social designing as email addresses are not publically shown on LinkedIn. Discovering people that once worked for the association are

- pag. 244

Kali Linux

incredible wellsprings of data if social designing is permitted by the ROE. At long last LinkedIn has begun to post openings for work on its site, making it possible to comprehend the advancements utilized at the objective association.

Make a Doppleganger

A doppelganger in old stories is a spooky duplicate of a person. It is normal practice to build up a persona before starting observation in the online life world. It is generally not a good idea to direct research on an objective utilizing the profile of a security master or entrance analyzer. A much better idea is if the infiltration analyzer can build up social connections with people from the association through online networking. It would be increasingly compelling if the infiltration analyzer had a persona that professed to have once worked in the objective association or went to a similar school as the CEO that the entrance analyzer is attempting to interface with on LinkedIn. Clearly the infiltration analyzer must be careful about totally assuming control over a genuine individual's personality, a demonstration that could lead some to accept that fraud has happened. it is conceivable for two individuals to have comparable names. For instance, building up a fictional persona with the name of John Smith that went to Wisconsin University and a foundation completely made up isn't equivalent to taking the personality of the real John Smith that went there. Regardless, make sure that your persona doesn't seep over into data fraud or misrepresentation. This implies, in addition to other things, not rounding out that Visa application that has your persona's name on it or utilizing this persona for going into lawful concurrences with the persona.

Kali Linux

The lines for utilizing a doppelganger ought to be indicated from the get-go in the commitment, and if social designing is permitted, the doppelganger ought to be built up that will be viable when social building becomes an integral factor. When rounding out enlistment for web-based life locales the infiltration analyzer should focus on the utilization approach to guarantee strategies, rules, or laws are not being broken by utilizing a doppelganger persona.

Places of Work

Looking through employment sites, like Monster, Career Builder, and Dice, can, occasionally, bring about intriguing discoveries. Like the objectives possess site, these sites can reveal insight into the innovations utilized at the objective site. Looking through these pages with the association being referred to will regularly bring about the places that should be filled, helping the infiltration analyzer better comprehend the objective. As of late, numerous organizations have started to comprehend this shortcoming and are currently posting situations as "organization private" or other proclamation in the activity postings.

DNS and DNS Attacks

Space Name Services, or DNS, gives tending to help to the Internet. By and large individuals have better memories recollecting and utilizing names, as Google.com, while PCs have a simpler time utilizing numbers like 173.194.46.19 (one of Google's locations). The various leveled structure of the Web additionally utilizes numbered octets progressively proficient. This creates an

Kali Linux

issue where the best plan for individuals doesn't coordinate the best plan for PCs. Name servers help to tackle this issue by filling in as interpreters between PCs and individuals.

These name servers are set up in a various leveled request with top-level space (TLD) servers, serving fundamental areas, such as .com, .gov, .edu, and numerous others. At the opposite finish of the name server chain of importance each system can have its very own name server that enables neighborhood administrations and PCs to be gotten to by name rather than by IP address.

Potentially the most effortless approach to comprehend the essential usefulness of name servers is to stroll through how a PC and internet browser collaborate and work with the whole name server framework. From the neighborhood name server to the root, or name server that is over the TLDs, each name server can inquiry the following name server above it or give data to the name server underneath it. In the event that the PC client was to type the location for Google into an internet browser a chain of occasions would be activated to decipher the intelligible name to one increasingly valuable to a PC. This begins with the client's PC asking the nearby name server in the event that it realizes the IP address identifies with www.google.com, if this name server has had this solicitation in the ongoing past and has reserved the appropriate response or Google was enrolled with that name server the IP address could be returned right away. If that name server doesn't have the data reserved, or generally put away, it asks the following name server, if it knows the data it is returned if not this

- pag. 247

Kali Linux

proceeds until the solicitation arrives at the TLD name server, for this situation the name server for.com.

Name servers contain a ton of helpful data, well past pages. For instance, the name server will contain the mail server, or MX record, for the area, other named PCs or "A" records and other supportive data.

Inquiry a Name Server

By their overall plan, most name servers are available to the general population. The following direction entered in the Kali Linux terminal will inquiry the name server appointed to the nearby PC.

nslookup

This will bring about a caret (.) being shown in the terminal demonstrating the framework is anticipating input. Type the following direction to question the neighborhood name server to decide the IP address of the Google site page. www.google.com

This will restore various IP tends to both definitive (the main reactions) and non-authoritative, those following the non-authoritative note.

Non-authoritative answers are an incredible wellspring of data as this term shows the data is given from the server's store.

Sifting Google look.

Kali Linux

To exit from nslookup utilize the accompanying order. exit

The nslookup direction will utilize the name server characterized for the nearby machine. To show the name servers being utilized for the current nslookup directions utilize the following order.
nslookup

. server

The order nslookup can return other data also. For instance, to scan for the entirety of the mail servers type the accompanying directions.

. set sort 5 MX

. google.com

This will restore the entirety of the known mail servers for the Google area. Distinguishing the various sorts of records about the objective can be a significant piece of finishing surveillance. As expressed earlier, the nslookup direction, as a matter of course, utilizes the privately characterized name server. In Kali Linux, the name server is characterized in the resolv.conf record situated in the/and so forth catalog. Use the following directions to recognize the privately characterized name server.

feline/and so forth/resolv.conf

Kali Linux

The name server utilized by nslookup can be changed to the objective area's name server. First recognize the objectives name server with the following direction.

nslookup

. set sort 5 ns

. google.com

When the objective name servers have been recognized, the name server utilized by nslookup can be changed to one of the objective's name servers utilizing the following order. This model sets the name server to one of Google's name servers.

nslookup

. server 216.239.32.10

There are various records that can be found utilizing nslookup.

Zone Transfer

While it is conceivable to increase a great deal of data by utilizing programs like nslookup to physically move data, it is conceivable to get significantly more data in a shorter time utilizing a zone move. A zone move actually dumps the entirety of the data from a name server. This procedure is helpful for refreshing approved name servers. Misconfigured name servers permit zone moves not

Kali Linux

exclusively to approved customers for refreshes, but anybody that demands the exchange.

The Domain Internet Gopher (DIG) is a program that can be utilized to endeavor zone moves. To endeavor a zone move utilize the following order.

burrow @[name server] [domain] axfr

Most moves will fizzle, in any case, if the objective name server is mis-configured.

The whole name servers record set will be moved to the neighborhood Kali Linux PC. When utilizing this direction, the space will be the area short any host, for instance, foo.com not www.foo.com. The axfr direction demonstrates burrow should demand a zone move. If the exchange is fruitful, the data shown can be utilized to add to the objective's profile. This will give important data for the future periods of the entrance test.

Kali Linux

Chapter 9: Scanning

After the infiltration analyzer has finished the surveillance period of an association, they will move into the examining stage. In this stage, the infiltration analyzer can take the data found out about the workers, temporary workers, and data frameworks to start extending the perspective on physical data framework structures inside the association. Like any of different stages in the infiltration testing lifecycle, the entrance analyzer can come back to previous stages as expected to acquire data to upgrade data accumulated in the checking stage.

The fundamental focal point of the filtering stage is to decide explicit data about the PCs and different gadgets that are associated with the focused-on system of the association. All through this stage, the emphasis is on deciding hub type (work area, PC, server, organize gadget, or versatile figuring stage), working framework, open administrations offered (web applications, SMTP, FTP, and so on.), and even potential vulnerabilities.

Vulnerabilities at this level are regularly alluded to as, "low hanging natural product."

Examining is finished with various devices; this section will concentrate on probably the best known and best devices including Nmap, Hping, and Nessus. The objective of this stage is to have a posting of potential focuses for the following period of the infiltration testing lifecycle: misuse.

Understanding Network Traffic

System traffic can be confounding to certain individuals; in any case, an essential comprehension of this theme is required to get the greatest profit by the examining stage. System traffic is the electronic correspondence that happens between PC frameworks that are associated by various strategies. Today the most widely recognized strategies for systems administration are Wired and Wireless Ethernet. Comprehension of the crucial standards of Ethernet correspondence is vital. This section will explore ports and firewalls, IP conventions including Transmission Control Protocol (TCP), Client Datagram Protocol (UDP), and Internet Control Management Protocol (ICMP).

Getting Ports and Firewalls

One of the most essential strategies for protecting a system is by actualizing a firewall between the inside, frequently corporate, organize and the remainder of the world, like the Internet. A firewall is just a registering gadget with at least two system cards filling in as a guardian for the system. Access control records carefully screen outbound traffic (departure) and inbound traffic (entrance). Only traffic that meets the criteria of the entrance controls is permitted to pass, while the rest are dropped by the firewall. It does this by opening or shutting ports to permit or deny traffic.

Ports are the distinctive correspondence channels utilized for PC to PC correspondence. There are 65,535 TCP ports and another 65,535 UDP ports that can be utilized for correspondence. A small

Kali Linux

number of these ports are assigned for a particular reason, but are not confined to this utilization. For instance, the TCP port 80 is frequently utilized for typical Internet web traffic using the Hypertext Transfer Protocol (HTTP), yet other traffic can go over port 80 and Internet traffic can be transmitted over different ports.

One approach is to consider ports as a huge place of business with entryways prompting various rooms. Every one of these rooms has an office staff that makes a particular showing and oversees various capacities. The workplace behind suite number 80 handles the website page demand that come in. It is workable for the web division to move to an alternate office, like the workplace in suite 8080, proceeding to do similar capacities, dealing with web demands, there. An alternate gathering could move into suite 80 that has nothing to do with the web demands or the suite could be essentially shut, bolted, and unused. Guests attempting to discover the web group would need to realize the web group is presently in suite 8080 and no longer in suite 80. A guest attempting to get web data from suite 80 after the web group has moved will be disillusioned and not get the required data as inappropriate people will be there or the workplace will be bolted, while a guest that has the right address will get the site page mentioned from the new office in suite 8080.

Understanding IP Protocols
Conventions are rules, even on PC systems. Lawmakers and significant level authorities regularly have staff individuals that handle convention issues. The individuals in convention workplaces ensure each guest or authority message is done in a way that

Kali Linux

guarantees the message or guest is gotten effectively, in the right organization and with the correct titles and respects.

In the PC world, these conventions guarantee correspondence between frameworks happens as indicated by predefined rules. While there is an amazingly high number of conventions accessible for all PC frameworks, this section will address three of the conventions most regularly utilized by prominent filtering applications on Kali Linux to use checking, defenselessness disclosure, and entrance testing: TCP, UDP, and ICMP.

TCP

One of the primary conventions utilized for organize interchanges is the TCP.

TCP is an association-based correspondence convention, implying that the PCs on each side of the interchanges channel recognize that the session is open and the messages are being gotten on each side of the association. Previously, numerous individuals have related this to a telephone call.

Conclusion

As you have completed this eBook, you can now easily create a very clear perception of the concepts of hacking along with the linked processes. You have also gained a lot of knowledge about the properties, functioning and usage of Kali Linux. After completing this book, you will be able to frame up all the necessary tools along with the components required for setting up a secure and safe server of network meant for your business or personal use. Always keep one thing in mind; you are the one who is responsible for everything that happens with your network or server.

With the help of Kali Linux and its relevant tools, you will have complete control over the interface of your network security. This eBook is not only about the aspects of Kali Linux, it also discusses the basics of networking along with its security. With the help of Kali Linux, you will be able to perform periodic penetration testing which will ultimately determine the security of your system.

So, if you are thinking about improving the security of your network server, then start right away with the help of this eBook along with Kali Linux. Remember, you are the one who can actually make or break the security wall of your network.

Kali Linux

If you find this book helpful for your business in any way, kindly leave a review on Amazon.

www.ingramcontent.com/pod-product-compliance
Lightning Source LLC
Chambersburg PA
CBHW071353210526
45465CB00001B/70